DATE DUE

DEMCO 38-296

Match Pointers

*Courtside with the
Winningest Coach in
Tennis History*

Dan Magill

LONGSTREET PRESS
Atlanta, Georgia

Published by
LONGSTREET PRESS, INC.
A subsidiary of Cox Newspapers,
A division of Cox Enterprises, Inc.
2140 Newmarket Parkway
Suite 118
Marietta, Georgia 30067

Printed in the United States of America

1st printing 1995

Library of Congress Catalog Card Number: 94-74233

ISBN 1-56352-194-6

This book was printed by Quebecor Printing, Kingsport, Tennessee

Film preparation by Holland Graphics, Mableton, Georgia

Jacket design by Jill Dible
Book design and typesetting by Laura McDonald

Table of Contents

To Rosemary . . .
and
to all my players, fans
and friends who made
Georgia's tennis record the best
of all sports
at all SEC schools
for the past quarter-century.

Introduction

WHAT IT TAKES TO BE A CHAMPION

The dictionary defines the word *champion* as "one who holds first place or wins first prize in a contest, superior to all others." It proceeds to give the word's derivation from the Middle English, Old French, West Germanic, and Latin. But it omits to delineate what it takes to be a champion.

Charley Trippi, the University of Georgia's triple-threat halfback of the 1940s, was voted the Southeastern Conference's greatest football player of its first 50 years and is a member of both the College and Professional Halls of Fame. Late in the 1946 season, Georgia and Alabama, both undefeated, met for a crucial game in Athens. In the first quarter, Alabama penned Georgia back on its own goal line, and Trippi dropped back to punt on third down. Alabama blocked the kick, and three 'Bama players dived for the loose ball. So did Trippi, and even though he got a late jump, he came out of the pile with the ball. Then, on fourth down, he punted out of danger and went on to lead Georgia to a great victory. *He had the determination of a champion.*

William David (Billy) Conn, the pride of Pittsburgh, was the greatest boxer I ever saw. He was 23 when he fought Joltin' Joe Louis, in his prime at 27, for the heavyweight title in the summer of 1941 at New York's old Polo Grounds. Conn had been the world's welterweight and middleweight champion, at a very young age, before winning the light-heavyweight crown. He weighed in at only 174 pounds (he was a true light-heavyweight) the day he fought Louis, who tipped the scales at 199 3/4. Both were trained down to the muscle and bone — not an ounce of fat anywhere.

Conn had never been defeated, never even been knocked down. The great sportswriter Grantland Rice wrote the day of the fight that Louis probably for the first time would be facing an opponent absolutely fearless and completely unafraid of the devastating punching power in both hands of the celebrated Brown Bomber from Detroit, who had knocked out almost every man he had met in the ring.

The experts agreed that Conn's only chance was to stay out of the way of the heavier and harder-hitting Louis, to use his superior speed afoot and defensive skills and possibly out-point the champion. But in the third round Louis maneuvered Conn into the corner, whence no Louis opponent in history had ever been able to escape. Once Joltin' Joe had his foe hemmed in, "church was out." But Joltin' Joe had never before met an opponent with the great fighting heart of Billy Conn, and instead of cowering in the face of Louis's barrage of blows, Conn retaliated by fighting his way out — throwing punches so fast and furiously that Louis was startled — and then dancing his way to the center of the ring. *Billy Conn had the heart of a champion.*

Conn then took control of the fight. He outpointed Louis the next nine rounds, and late in the 12th round he staggered Louis with a left hook, then crossed with a right to the head that floored the Brown Bomber, who was luckily saved by the bell. Sensing a knockout within his grasp, Conn didn't even sit on his stool during the rest period, and when the bell rang for the 13th round, he ran to finish off his opponent. But he was a little careless in resuming his attack; Louis saw an opening and instinctively tagged Conn on the chin with his dynamite left jab. Conn was stunned and dropped both arms. Louis then pummeled his opponent with a torrent of sledgehammer blows, but Conn would not go down. Finally

Louis approached from Conn's side and virtually chopped and shoved him down, at which point referee Arthur Donovan stopped one of the greatest fights in ring history. *Joe Louis had the sheer power and prowess of a champion.*

Of course, I've seen many great tennis champions, and I've noted the many qualities that tennis champions possess. First is God-given talent: both racquet talent and such innate physical skills as agility, strength, stamina, good vision, quick reflexes and speed afoot.

But along with physical prowess, a champion must have qualities of mind and character. Becoming a champion takes the ability to concentrate throughout the match without ever getting distracted or discouraged. It takes the utmost in determination, dedication, and commitment to hard work. And it takes an unyielding, indomitable, fighting spirit — the heart of a lion.

I'd prefer my champion to be a splendid sportsman, too, and I think the majority of champions are fine sportsmen. Some of the greatest champions have been sorry sportsmen, to say the least, but it's interesting to note that the only two men ever to win tennis's Grand Slam, J. Donald Budge of the United States and Rodney Laver of Australia, were not only supreme champions but also outstanding sportsmen.

When Mikael Pernfors won the NCAA singles in 1984, most people (including me) thought he would turn professional (as was the trend then) instead of returning for his final season of eligibility. But Mikael told me, "I want to come back. I want us to win the team title next year, and we can do it." He did return, he repeated as singles champion, and — more importantly to him — he led us to the team title, too.

The most sought-after recruit in the country in 1987 was Al Parker of Claxton, Ga., who had won a record 25 USTA junior titles. I was jubilant when he signed a Georgia grant-in-aid. He got off to a flying start his first quarter of school in the fall of '87, winning the tough Southern Collegiates and the ITCA Region Three Indoors. But in January, in the SEC Indoors at Tuscaloosa, he went down with a back injury that knocked him out of play for the next three months.

When he was given permission to play again, I told him, "Al, we only have a couple of weeks left on the schedule. You can't possibly regain top form. I think it best that you be declared a 'hardship case' due to your injury, and you won't lose a year of eligibility."

Al replied, "All of us want very much to win the SEC team tournament. It's going to be close. I may not be able to win my division, but I might score a point or two that would help make the difference."

Well, Al was not anywhere near top form, but he earned one point at No. 1 singles and one more point at No. 1 doubles, and we won the team title by two points, edging hometown favorite Kentucky, 20-18.

Mikael and Al were champion players and champion people, too.

It is ideal for a tennis champion to possess all the shots and be able to win from the back court and at the net. Big Bill Tilden was the finest all-court player in his day; today Pete Sampras is a perfect example of a champion all-court player — a master of many shots with amazing power, too. But there have been many champions who did not have an all-court game. Ivan Lendl became world's champion without being strong at the net. Stefan Edberg became world's champion on the strength of a great topspin serve and a crunching volley. Bryan (Bitsy) Grant, probably the South's greatest player ever, was a backcourt battler and defensive retriever extraordinaire. Bjorn Borg was world's champion mainly because of his great athletic ability and incomparable backcourt game. Jimmy Connors was a backcourt slugger with a knockout punch on his two-handed backhand side. John McEnroe was a serve-and-volley genius.

But regardless of the relative strengths and weaknesses of their games, all of these players had *the essential spirit of a champion.*

In 1976, the SEC's first indoor tournament was held at LSU. I thought we'd win it. Our No. 1 man, Charlie Ellis, had sat out the previous year after having transferred from Georgia Southern, and he was chomping at the bit, anxious to do his part in bringing home the team title. He gained the finals and led Gary Albertine of LSU 6-4, 6-6, and 4-2 in the nine-point tie-breaker (meaning he had *triple match point* and he was serving to boot).

On his first serve at 4-2 in the breaker, Charlie hit a good one to Albertine's weaker forehand side and drew a fat set-up, but Charlie "Big-Iked" the volley a foot deep, making it 4-3. On the next point, Albertine hit a blistering backhand passing shot, tying the score at 4-4. At this point I yelled to Charlie, "Get the first serve to his forehand," which he did, resulting in another set-up return. This time Charlie didn't "Big-Ike" the volley; instead he played it too safe, and Albertine burned him with a fine passing shot to take the set. Albertine went on to win the third set, and Georgia lost the team title by one point, 19-18.

On the trip back home, nobody took the loss harder than Charlie, a super competitor. He swore to me that he'd do better next year and get sweet revenge, which he did. He returned to Baton Rouge in '77, won both the singles and doubles and led us to the team championship, too. *There was a champion.*

Champions are at their best when the chips are down and the pressure is turned up, and nowhere in tennis is the pressure greater than when playing for one's country in Davis Cup matches. Two of the greatest were the Don Budge-Gottfried von Cramm match in the 1937 U.S.-Germany tie and the Stan Smith-Ion Tiriac battle in the 1972 U.S.-Romania final round tie at Bucharest.

The Budge-von Cramm five-set classic was played on grass at Wimbledon because the winning team was to meet Cup-holding Great Britain on the same courts a few days later. It was the last match of the tie; the teams were even at two matches apiece. With Fred Perry having turned pro, Budge and von Cramm were the two finest amateurs in the world. Budge had beaten von Cramm on the same grass earlier in the summer in the Wimbledon finals, and von Cramm had been runner-up three straight years at Wimbledon, losing to Perry in 1935 and '36 and to Budge in '37. Von Cramm won the first two sets, 8-6, 7-5, but Budge fought back to take the third and fourth, 6-4, 6-2. Then the great German went ahead 4-1 in the fifth and final set, but Budge fought back and finally triumphed 8-6. Bitsy Grant, who was there and who later described it to me, was among the many who considered this match the greatest ever in Davis Cup history.

The brilliant Ilie Nastase and colorful Ion Tiriac had almost won the Cup for Romania in 1971, losing to the U.S., 3-2, at Charlotte, N.C., in a match that I saw. In 1972, they were on their home courts in Bucharest, facing Stan Smith and Tom Gorman in singles, and Smith and Eric Van Dillen in doubles. Smith beat Nastase the first day, and Smith and Van Dillen avenged the previous year's loss to Nastase and Tiriac in doubles. But Gorman lost both of his singles matches, setting up a final match for the Cup between Smith and Tiriac. The two men took the court before 12,000 screaming partisan Romanians, who U.S. captain Dennis Ralston told me were the most hostile fans he had ever seen. But the big Californian was able to keep his cool and win another fantastic five-setter, 4-6, 6-2, 6-4, 2-6, 6-0.

With their talent, their grit, their guts, their drive to succeed, and their indomitable spirit, *Don Budge and Stan Smith were champions.*

Match
Pointers

"Different Strokes"

THE DREADED DROP SHOT

The dreaded drop shot is certainly an effective weapon when used at the right time and with the necessary element of disguise.

Early in my career I lost a big junior match when my opponent utilized the drop shot to lure me to the net to take advantage of my practically nonexistent volley and overhead. I was a classic victim of the drop shot that day.

The match happened to be in the state junior tournament in Atlanta in the late 1930s. My opponent was the reigning Southern Boys' 18 champion, Cortez Suttles of East Point. I was winning most of the points in long baseline rallies on slow red clay courts, which caused Cortez' coach, Bill Lufler (the first teaching pro in Atlanta, I believe), to send instructions to his protégé to use the drop shot to bring me to the net and then either to pass or lob over me. This tactic worked to perfection. Even when I had a chance to volley, I would hit a set-up, and I messed up numerous lobs with my overhead errors. I was never in the match from that point on.

Bill Lufler went on to a most distinguished career as a coach at both Presbyterian College and the University of Miami. He is also in the Collegiate Tennis Hall of Fame. In the early 1950s King Gustav invited Bill to Sweden to establish the junior development program that has been primarily responsible for Sweden turning out so many great players.

Incidentally, when Bill was in Athens in 1985 to be inducted into the Collegiate Hall of Fame, it was my honor to introduce him, and I mentioned the details of my junior match against his protégé back in 1939, adding that I doubted Bill would remember it.

But when Bill came to the podium, he got a big laugh by saying, "Do I remember your match against Cortez Suttles? How could I ever forget it! You were the most unorthodox, most countrified shotmaker I have ever seen on a tennis court to this day."

But I did profit by that hard lesson I learned in 1939. I learned how to anticipate the drop shot and the kind of retaliatory shots to make. Of course, it's no problem if you get to the drop shots in plenty of time; then you can win the point with a variety of shots. But if you barely get to the drop shot, you must attempt a defensive shot, usually deep straight ahead so that a quick recovery can be made at the proper net position.

Strangely, I never once thought about developing a drop shot myself until I was in my late thirties, playing state champion Don Floyd (father of former U.S. Wightman Cup and Federation Cup captain Donna Floyd Fales) in the Georgia State Men's Open in the late 1950s on clay at the Bitsy Grant Center in Atlanta. It was a semifinal match and Don prevailed, 6-4, 6-4.

After this match, Don gave me some good advice: "Dan, I've been watching you play a number of years and you don't have a single shot with which you can earn the point. You're just hoping to outsteady your opponent. You need a shot

Billie Jean comes to pay homage to the drop shot (l-r: Coach Manuel Diaz, Allen Miller, Coach Jeff Wallace, Billie Jean King, Jack Frierson, Dan Magill).

that will end the point in your favor, and I recommend that you work on the drop shot, which can easily be developed off a chop stroke — just the kind you use off both sides."

Don then demonstrated how to hit the drop shot by blocking the ball with a chop stroke, simply stopping the stroke upon contact. He also said I could get good disguise because my opponent could not discern until the last moment whether I was going to hit a chop-stroke drive or a drop shot.

I went back to Athens and experimented with the drop shot, and, sure enough, it was easy for me to acquire a satisfactory one without a whole lot of practice. It was natural for me with my chop-stroke style. In fact, there is no doubt that the drop shot has become my best shot and has helped me win some state and Southern senior titles.

Some years ago there was a poll among players, ranking the best shotmakers in the South, and I won in the drop shot category. The great Billie Jean King heard about this when she visited her brother Randy Moffitt (one-time San Francisco Giants pitcher) in Athens at Christmastime 1993.

I had arranged a doubles match for Billie Jean at our indoor courts. She and former Georgia player Jack Frierson played several sets against Georgia women's coach Jeff Wallace and former Georgia NCAA doubles champion Allen Miller, following which I told Billie Jean that she had the best volleying form I had ever seen, man or woman.

A few minutes later, as I was getting ready to leave the building, Allen Miller hollered to me, "Hey, Coach, Billie Jean wants to see your dreaded drop shot."

Billie Jean added with a smile, "Yeah, Coach Magill, it would be a shame if I came all the way to Athens and didn't get a look at one of the world's greatest shots."

I knew she was teasing me, but I grabbed a racquet and had Coach Wallace feed a ball to my forehand, following which I hit a perfect drop shot that landed barely over the net, right in front of Billie Jean.

"How about the backhand?" Billie Jean said. So Coach Wallace fed the ball to my backhand, and I hit another perfect drop shot that hardly bounced. Billie Jean laughed and said, "Fantastic! Best I ever saw!"

I tossed the racquet back to Allen Miller and yelled back to Billie Jean as I went out the door, "Come back next year and I'll show you my drop-shot serve and drop-shot overhead."

THE BIG FOREHAND

There is nothing more decisive or more beautiful than a clean-cut forehand drive with "put-away" placement. It is the *coup de grace* of tennis shots, and there have been many players who were gifted in its execution — from the days of Little Bill Johnston and Big Bill Tilden right on up to Andre Agassi and Jim Courier of today.

The most spectacular Bulldog forehand ever, in my opinion, was owned by the lanky middle-Georgian, Norman King Carter III of Butler, down in Taylor County. "Trey" was the son of a country schoolteacher and coach, who had played basketball at Clemson and Mercer. Trey also was a cousin of the 39th president of the United States, James Earl Carter.

Although he never made All-America, he was a three-time All-SEC selection and one of the most valuable players ever to wear the Red and Black. Trey helped us win three SEC and two NCAA team titles. In addition, he won the tough Princeton Indoors twice (almost thrice, losing a three-set finals match), and he is the only player ever to capture the Georgia State Collegiate singles four times: 1985-86-87-88.

It was in the State Collegiates as a freshman that Trey unknowingly scored the greatest victory of his career. I didn't play our "big guns" (Mikael Pernfors, George Bezecny and Allen Miller), resting them for the upcoming NCAAs; and Trey upset his teammate Philip Johnson to reach the finals against a young Dutchman from Armstrong State in Savannah, Paul Haarhuis, who had upset the No. 1 seed, Georgia's Deane Frey, in the semis. None of us had ever heard of Haarhuis, and I even censured Trey for not hustling against him. So before the finals, I warned Carter not to loaf against this unknown player. Well, Trey won a hard-fought three-setter, 3-6, 7-5, 6-3, following which I jumped on him for not hustling in the first set.

To which Trey retorted: "Coach, I never tried harder in all my life to win a match. That guy is a terrific player."

It turned out that Haarhuis was a terrific talent. A few years later he knocked off John McEnroe in the U.S. Open, and today he is among the top players in the world. He won the Australian and U.S. doubles in 1994.

Trey's most pleasing victory as a Georgia player, however

Trey Carter gets a big win in the 1985 NCAA Championships.

—one that immortalized him with Bulldog fans — came during doubles competition. He and T. J. Middleton, who in 1993 led the Wichita Advantage to the World Team Tennis title, won the deciding doubles match to topple mighty Southern California in the semifinals of the 1987 NCAA team tournament.

The proud Trojans had come to Athens undefeated, riding

high on a 32-match winning streak, and they were especially looking forward to smashing Georgia, which had upset them four straight times in the NCAAs during the 1980s. This year, USC's future NCAA doubles champions Rick Leach and Scott Melville quickly won at No. 1 doubles to put USC out front, 4-3. A few minutes later, though, the team score was knotted at 4-all when Georgia's outstanding No. 3 tandem, Philip Johnson and freshman Jim Childs, triumphed.

Now the spotlight shifted to the showdown on the center court, drawing full attention of the overflow crowd of 5,000 partisan Georgia fans. USC had been heavily favored to win this particular doubles match, claiming the nation's best No. 2 team in big Luke Jensen (later to win the French Open doubles) and Eric Amend (later to win the NCAA doubles). But Georgia had a very good team, too, in a pair of cool "clutch" players (Carter and Middleton) whom I had nicknamed our "swat team." And they played like fiends to score a 7-5, 6-3 victory. Carter's fantastic forehand service returns helped get several crucial service breaks.

I never will forget the first time I saw Trey Carter hit his fabulous forehand drive in early September 1984, during his first practice with the Georgia team. It was a most unorthodox, severe Western forehand. He could get plenty of topspin and could also wallop the most powerful flat forehand putaway I had ever seen when he took the ball at the top of the bounce.

I remember asking Trey at the time, "Who taught you that forehand?"

"Nobody," he answered, which I certainly believed. Most super shots are natural, and many of them are unorthodox. Trey further stated, "Rob Cadwallader [former Mississippi State star and a native of Australia] was my first teacher when I was 11 years old. My dad took me over to Callaway Gardens, not far from Butler, where Rob was the pro. He taught me to grip the racquet by trying to shake hands with it. But I didn't feel at home with it and never could hit the ball well with his recommended grip. So I'd go back to my old grip and did so much better with it that Rob finally told me just to 'do it my way.'"

Boy, am I glad that Rob Cadwallader was smart enough not to mess up the most spectacular forehand I ever saw!

THE "BIG IKE" OVERHEAD

The overhead is one of the most spectacular shots in tennis, especially when the player is pushed back deep by a high lob and has to jump to make the smash. It takes a good athlete to execute the jumping overhead smash.

Five of the best we ever had at Georgia were Norman Holmes, Manuel Diaz, Charlie Ellis, Brent Crymes, and little Danny Birchmore, who precisely angled his overheads, relying on accuracy rather than the power employed by the others.

Raymond Charles Ellis, a strapping six-two Indiana Hoosier from New Albany, was my most unforgettable exponent of the overhead smash. He also was one of the most colorful characters ever to play in the Southeastern Conference and a fighting competitor nonpareil.

Although he walked with a slight limp, the result of having had polio as a boy, he could run and jump like an antelope. Charlie was a very aggressive player. He loved to take the net on his serve or on his beautiful, classical, sliced-backhand approach. But his favorite shot was the overhead smash, for which he always jumped high — even when it was unnecessary to jump — to put the ball away. He relished bouncing it over the fence, even when that feat was both unnecessary and bothersome. He epitomized the term "Big Ike," given players who prefer to knock the heck out of the ball instead of winning the point with a simple placement.

Charlie won many big matches for Georgia, including the SEC Indoor No. 1 singles and doubles in 1977, the SEC Outdoor No. 1 doubles in 1977, the Georgia State Collegiate singles in 1976 and doubles in 1976–77, and the Princeton Indoor doubles in 1977.

Some of his best play was in the NCAAs at Corpus Christi in 1976 and in Athens in 1977. At Corpus Christi in the third round he played a close 6-4, 6-4 match against top seed Peter Fleming of UCLA; and he and David Dick extended the No. 3 doubles seeds, Pat DuPre and Bill Maze of Stanford to 6-4, 3-6, 6-3, also in the third round.

In Athens his senior year he hustled and battled his way into the NCAA singles quarterfinals, losing a tight three-setter to the ultimate finalist, Tony Graham of UCLA, 6-1, 3-6, 6-4. In the same tournament, Charlie and Wesley Cash, who were seeded sixth in the doubles, had high hopes of perhaps winning the title. They had won three big tournaments during the season, without dropping a set: the SEC Indoors and Outdoors and the Princeton Indoors.

But in the very first round they came up against Big 10 champions Jeff Etterbeck and Jud Shaufler of Michigan. Charlie and Wes took the first set in a tie-breaker and battled their way to match point in the second set. They were in winning position at the net when Etterbeck threw up a high lob, forcing Charlie all the way back to the baseline, at which point Charlie made his patented leap for his "Big Ike" overhead smash.

I was sitting in the grandstand corner, smack on the line, and yelled to Charlie, "Let it go!"

It was clearly going to be out by at least a foot, but Charlie couldn't resist going for his favorite shot. This time, however, he did something he seldom did: he missed it, knocking it into the net.

I murmured to myself, "Goddamned Big Ike shot!"

Charlie Ellis prepares to "Big Ike" the overhead (as Wesley Cash looks on).

Charlie shot me a "daggers" look and hissed, "You made me miss my shot when you hollered."

Unfortunately, Charlie and Wes went on to lose this toughly contested match, 6-7, 7-6, 7-5.

Despite his anger at that moment, we remained good friends. Several years later he asked me to recommend him for the head pro job at the Lexington (Ky.) Racquet Club, which I happily did — and he got the job, too. But I didn't mention one word about Charlie's finest shot: the Big Ike overhead smash.

THE FINE ART OF THE VOLLEY

Lecturers on the volley say that one should "punch" or "block" the ball to execute this shot effectively. Former Southern Methodist coach, NCAA champion, and Wimbledon doubles king Dennis Ralston was the best teacher and demonstrator of the volley I ever heard, and he always said one should "pop" the ball in making this all-important stroke that so often finishes off the point.

Dennis certainly could "pop" his volley. He won the Wimbledon doubles (with Rafael Osuna) when he was only eighteen years old, and he won the NCAA doubles and singles twice for Southern Cal, with volleying playing a huge part in his success.

It's important to acknowledge the variety of effective volleys. Of course there's the severe volley, the one smacked away for a winner. But there's also the drop or stop volley, which is a deadly weapon to have when your opponent is behind the baseline and you have good net position. And there's also the lob volley, a delicate shot used effectively in doubles when all four players are at the net.

Finally, there's the defensive volley, an underrated but very important shot, and I used to devote a lot of time to practice drills on it. Usually, it should be hit back deep with a good margin of error.

In my early days of coaching it was recommended that

young players learn the backcourt game first and move on to volleying and the net game only after the ground strokes were mastered. Nowadays, many pros teach the volley from the beginning, right along with the ground strokes, and I agree with this new philosophy. I think it is important for players to learn quickly that ground strokes and volleys are very different strokes. In executing ground strokes, of course, the player has more time to make both a longer stroke and a follow-through; a player at the net generally has time for only a very short stroke, and he doesn't need a long stroke or follow-through to get pace on the ball. A player properly "popping" the volley gets plenty of pace off his opponent's ball.

I've had many fine volleyers at Georgia. Some, like Lindsey Hopkins III, Manuel Diaz, Bill Rogers, Bob Tanis, Rocky Huffman and T. J. Middleton (finalist in the 1994 Wimbledon mixed doubles with Lori McNeil) were severe volleyers. They could powerfully dispatch the ball for clean winners. Others, like Allen Miller in particular, were finesse volleyers with a lot of touch, à la John McEnroe. Miller was also the best "poacher" at the net I ever had, particularly with his long lefthanded reach on the forehand side. He had a sixth sense at the net and never fouled up when he attempted to poach.

The most severe volleyer, both forehand and backhand, I ever had at Georgia was Bob Tanis, a native of Wayne, N.J., who was a solid, husky six-one. (He favored the continental grip on both sides, incidentally, unlike most players who change grips from forehand to backhand.) We nicknamed him "Big Bob" because he hit such booming volleys and service returns. He starred on Georgia teams that won the SEC round-robin all four of his years: 1970–73. He was a very good singles player, alternating at No. 1 his senior season, and in 1986 he won the USTA 35 hardcourt singles.

But I thought he was even better in doubles, where he could exploit his great volleying prowess. He won the tough

Volleying machine Bob Tanis.

Southern Collegiate doubles three straight years: 1970 and 1971 with Danny Birchmore and 1972 with lefthander Gordon Smith. He and Birchmore also won the fast Princeton Indoor doubles in 1972.

The finest volleying exhibition I ever saw in collegiate play was put on by Big Bob in the 1973 NCAA singles championships at Princeton. It was in the second round against a high-seeded player, All-American Freddie McNair of North Carolina — no mean volleyer himself — who later won the French Open doubles with Sherwood Stewart of Lamar State. Bob was certainly good enough to upset McNair, or almost any other player in the tourney; but with his incredible performance this day he didn't just upset McNair, he crushed him 6-1, 6-0.

Several factors contributed to this amazingly lopsided win. In the first place, McNair had a good first serve but only an average second serve, and on this day he rarely got in his first serve. So Big Bob had a field day knocking McNair's second serve down his throat time and again, enabling him to break serve five of six times.

On the other hand, Bob had a hot day with his first serve. It wasn't a great one, but it was good enough to let him get to the net, where his first volleys were so lethal. Consequently, Bob held all seven of his service games.

Another important factor was that rain forced the match indoors that day, where the hard-surfaced courts were much faster than the slow clay courts outdoors. This bit of help from Mother Nature really put Bob in the briar patch for his strong volleying game.

Finally, I believe all of Bob's kinfolks from his home in nearby Wayne were in the stands giving him a huge ovation every time he blasted a volley winner.

LEFTHANDERS, SOUTHPAWS & PORTSIDERS

Those players who hit the ball from the wrong side — lefthanders or southpaws or portsiders — have certainly done well in tennis from the very beginning, starting with that tall southpaw from St. Louis, Mo., who won the NCAAs for Harvard in 1899 and originated the international team competition that bears his name: Dwight F. Davis.

There have been plenty of other famous lefthanders, those who hold the most Grand Slam titles being Rodney Laver, Jimmy Connors and John McEnroe.

I especially appreciate lefthanders because I seldom had a team without one during my 34 years as Georgia's coach, and they helped us win many honors. And I'm not even including my very first protégé from the portside: M. B. Wheeler, an Athens boy whom I "coached" when he was only 14 and I was a "mature" 18, managing Georgia's old red clay courts just prior to World War II.

I'm also not including the last southpaw I claim as "my boy," Jack Frierson, another Athens lad who began his Georgia career as a freshman in 1989, the year after I retired as coach, but whom I had signed to a scholarship the previous year. Jack was taught by his father, Joe Frierson, Sr., who learned some fine points of tennis from me when he was my sparring partner during the 1960s and 1970s. So, indirectly, Jack was my protégé, too. Furthermore, his mother Ann was my secretary for years, but she "quit" me when Jack and his twin brother, Joe Jr., were born.

Both M. B. and Jack were top-notch players. We nick-named M. B. "Monkey Butt" because he wouldn't tell us what his initials stood for. Monkey Butt had a fantastic backhand crosscourt drive, hit flat with terrific pace. Jack won the national interscholastic singles and was a standout on two of Coach Manuel Diaz's teams that were finalists in the NCAA Team Tournament — 1989 and 1991.

A third Athens boy, Adam Yoculan, is a southpaw with a bright future right now. He is the son of Georgia's super gymnastics coach, Suzanne Yoculan, and when Adam becomes a champion I'll claim him, too, because I gave him a few tips when he first took up the game.

My second Georgia team in 1956 had two lefthanders: Don Hartsfield of Atlanta and the appropriately named LeeRoy Forehand of Cordele, Ga. Two years later we had three lefties: John Foster, a Connecticut Yankee; Hartsfield; and Richard Courts of Atlanta.

John Foster was probably the best singles player of all the fine lefthanders I coached. Sturdily built and standing five-nine, John attended prep school at Choate in Connecticut and wore the Red and Black in 1958 and 1959.

In his day North Carolina had the best tennis program in the South. Carolina was one of the few schools that gave tennis scholarships, and John went to Chapel Hill on a scholarship and played No.1 for the Tar Heels as a soph in 1957. But his good friend and Tar Heel teammate Dudley Baird, of Augusta, Ga., whom I had tried to recruit when he had won our Crackerland junior tournament, suddenly decided that he wanted to transfer to his native state's university. Out of a clear sky, Dudley wrote me that he and his friend John Foster were transferring to Georgia and wanted to come out for the tennis team in September 1957.

John played No.1 in singles and doubles both his years at Georgia. He and Lindsey Hopkins gave us one of the best 1-2 punches in the country in singles, and also one of the best doubles teams. They were finalists in the SEC No.1 doubles in both 1958 and 1959, losing to Tulane when the Greenies were the best in the country. In 1959 Foster and Hopkins extended the NCAA champions, Ron Holmberg and Crawford Henry, to 6-3, 9-7.

John lost to only two opponents that spring of 1959, All-Americans Ron Holmberg of Tulane and Ned Neely of Georgia Tech and he went three sets with both of them. I believe he would have beaten both of them had he only lobbed a few times when Holmberg and Neely took the net on him, which they had to do to win. But John persisted in trying to drive through them even though they usually had commanding position at the net. John explained to me that he thought it was "sissy" to throw up a lob.

John's greatest shot was his tremendous looping topspin forehand which could take his opponent into the next county when he hit his favored crosscourt drive.

In 1962, three years after his graduation from Georgia, John beat me in the finals of the Georgia State Men's singles in Atlanta when I was 41. The day before the match, an *Atlanta Constitution* sportswriter, who had never seen John play, asked him in an interview what he thought about playing his old coach. John quipped, "I'll take it easy on him. I can beat him lefthanded." That statement was printed the next day.

Jim Causey, Jr., of Davidson, N.C., and Mack Crenshaw, Jr., of Jacksonville, Fla., were outstanding southpaws on our 1964 team. Causey had the best flat overhead smash of any of our portsiders, and Big Mack, who stood six-seven, had the hardest flat cannonball serve. We give two annual awards in their memory: the Jim Causey Overhead Award and the Mack Crenshaw Big Serve Award.

Two Northwest Georgians, Gordon Smith of Rome (1972–75) and Bill Rogers of Marietta (1978–81) helped Georgia win many SEC team titles, and they were especially strong in doubles — Smith with his sliced serve and Rogers with his booming backhand volley.

Lefthander Paul Groth of Decatur, Ga., who starred for three years (1979–81), was one of the best athletes we ever had. At the same time we had big John Mangan, who made All-America with Bill Rogers in 1981 when they almost won the NCAAs. They formed the only lefthanded doubles team I ever coached. Incidentally, I don't believe an all-lefthanded team has ever won the NCAA doubles, and I think the great redheads, John McEnroe and Mark Woodforde (of Australia) are the only all-southpaw pair ever to win a Grand Slam doubles diadem: the U.S. Open in 1989.

The lithe Allen Miller of Tucker, Ga., was the finest all-round lefthander I ever coached. He was a wonderful all-court player without any weaknesses. He made All-America four straight years (1982–85) and won the NCAA doubles with Ola Malmqvist in 1983.

Joe Heldmann of Warren, N.J., was a great lefthanded prospect for Georgia in 1983 (he had won the USTA Boys' 18 Indoor singles), but he played only one year for us. He lost his life the next year in a tragic automobile accident in

Lotsa lefties: of these four players (l-r: John Mangan, Bill Rogers, Brent Crymes, Paul Groth), only Crymes is a righthander.

Mexico City that also took the life of former Pepperdine star John van Nostrand. We have an award in Big Joe's memory, too: the Joe Heldmann Lefthander Award.

Guess who has been my main sparring partner the past 10 years? He is Professor Bob Settles of the UGA School of Education, a lefthander who hits his forehand like John

Foster, his backhand like M. B. Wheeler, and his backhand volley like Bill Rogers. He's also the best lefthanded umpire in the NCAA tournament.

And guess who's the current chairman of the NCAA Tennis Committee? None other than that rugged southpaw from New Zealand, Wake Forest coach Ian Crookenden, who won the NCAA doubles for UCLA with both Arthur Ashe and Charley Pasarell.

Coach Crookenden can beat me lefthanded, too.

THE BIG SERVE OF
BIG MACK CRENSHAW, JR.

If McCarthy Crenshaw, Jr., had been able to play tennis the year round, he would have been an all-time Georgia great. But he played only in the spring, since he was also the first-string center on the basketball team. He had the most powerful service of any player I ever coached. He stood six-seven and hit a lefthanded cannonball. I well recall his acing Northwestern's All-Americans Martin Riessen and Clark Graebner (later U.S. Davis Cup stars) four straight points in a doubles match at Henry Feild Stadium in 1964.

Twenty-five years later, when Riessen and Graebner returned to Athens to be inducted into the Collegiate Tennis Hall of Fame, both of them asked me what had happened to the big lefthander who had aced them four straight points. I replied that he had become a judge, and they said, "Well, that judge had the hardest serve of anyone we ever played — Wimbledon and Davis Cup matches included."

Georgia did not give tennis scholarships during my first 11 years as coach (1955 through 1965), and I had to rustle up good players however I could. Big Mack was not the first basketball player I talked into playing tennis. The first was another lefthander, Don Hartsfield, whom I noticed practicing on our varsity courts one day in the early spring of 1956. Don accepted my invitation to try out for the team and developed into a winning player at the bottom of the line-up. He still plays in state senior tournaments and has been a generous supporter of our program.

Hartsfield had not played much tennis, but Crenshaw had been an outstanding player in the fast Florida Boys' competition. He also was extremely talented in baseball. In fact, he was considered a big league prospect during his high school days, and later, when he played tennis at Georgia, several major league scouts told me he ought to give up tennis and play baseball at Georgia. He had been a tremendous home run hitter and was the ideal first baseman: lefthanded and six-foot-seven.

But I "stole" young Mack from my good friend, Georgia baseball coach Jim Whatley. I had known young Mack's father, McCarthy Crenshaw, Sr., when he was an end on Georgia's football team and captain of the track team in the early 1930s, and I knew that young Mack would have to make a choice between tennis and baseball when he came to college. So I took advantage of my longtime friendship with Mack Sr. to get young Mack to choose tennis.

I'll never forget a match Mack played against Georgia Tech's ace, Duke Douglas, in the 1963 Georgia State Collegiates. Big Mack had 13 match points but lost, 8-10, 9-7, 12-10, in a three-hour-and-twenty-minute marathon. He was disgusted at blowing all those match points, but he was a great competitor; he and Chuck Harris exacted some measure of revenge by beating Douglas and George Dickinson in the finals of the doubles. A lesser person would have broken his racquets and given up the game for good.

NORMAN HOLMES'
"DON BUDGE" BACKHAND

Norman Holmes, Jr., was a tennis prodigy. His father, Norman Holmes, Sr., longtime teaching pro in Melbourne, Fla., put a racquet in his son's right hand as soon as he learned to walk. He won the Orange Bowl Boys' 11 division when he was only nine, and he usually topped the rankings in the fast Florida junior competition.

When I first saw Norman play as a Georgia freshman in September 1967, I asked him if he realized that he hit his backhand just like Don Budge (with his thumb up the racquet handle, bracing his grip, instead of wrapped around the handle).

He replied, "My dad taught me to hit it like Budge because he thought Budge had the best backhand ever."

Four years later, NCAA champion Jeff Borowiak of UCLA thought he was playing Don Budge in the fourth round of the 1971 NCAA singles at Notre Dame when Norman took the second set off him and almost scored a stunning upset. Only a tremendous effort by Borowiak to keep the ball away from Norm's beautiful backhand in the third set saved the big Bruin star that day.

Although only five-eight, Norm was sturdily built and as agile and strong an athlete as we ever had at Georgia. Despite a knee injury that handicapped him throughout his career, he made All-SEC four straight years. He not only had a super backhand, but a powerful topspin serve, a great overhead, and an excellent lob.

He was also a wonderful leader of our team when we were beginning to emerge as a Southern power. During Norm's junior year, we lost our opening dual match to Florida State in Tallahassee, then won all the rest — 23 straight matches (including revenge over FSU). We were unbeaten in the SEC round-robin, upsetting powerful Tennessee, 5-4, in

Norman Holmes and the infamous "spaghetti" racquet.

Knoxville. But the Vols beat us in the SEC tournament by one point, 22-21. Norm took the loss worse than anybody; he had been the top seed in the No. 1 singles, but he was upset in the very first round by Greg Hilley of Florida.

A few days later Norm came to my office with fire in his eyes, declaring that he would personally see to it that we won the title in 1971. Although he suffered another tough blow when he lost his No. 1 spot on our team to young Danny Birchmore, he definitely made good on his word. At the SEC tournament that year, he won the No. 2 singles, Birchmore won at No. 1, and he and Danny teamed for the No. 1 doubles. We won our first-ever conference championship, scoring 34 out of a possible 36 points.

Norm did well on the pro tour, reaching the third round of the U.S. Open in 1971 and the third round at Wimbledon in '73. He became one of the foremost exponents of the "spaghetti" racquet, mastering its use so expertly that he was predicted to move into the world's top ten. This type of racquet, with its double stringing, imparted incredible topspin to the ball — so incredible, in fact, that it was outlawed. Otherwise, there may have been no stopping Norman Holmes, whose beautiful backhand would have made Budge himself proud.

THE LOVELY LOB

I believe it takes a true tennis aficionado to fully appreciate the lovely lob. But mastery of this subtle stroke is crucial to success in tennis. Its "sissy" image among inexperienced players no doubt comes from its primary use as a defensive shot. But players who can't play good defense when defense is called for won't go far in this sport.

And of course, experienced players realize that the lob can also be a devastating offensive weapon. There may be no more satisfying shot than the perfectly executed offensive lob — stroked with topspin to bring the ball down hard and make it hop out of reach of the player who is helplessly hauling butt from the net back to the baseline. This shot not only beats your opponent; it beats him up.

Probably the best lobber we ever had at Georgia was Bill Shippey of Atlanta, who was awarded our very first full scholarship back in 1966. (I couldn't resist the nickname "Scholarshippey," but luckily it didn't catch on.) Bill was superb with both the defensive and offensive lobs, and he could disguise his offensive lob extremely well. Each year we give the Bill Shippey Lob Award to the Georgia player most proficient with this vitally important shot.

Few players ever had a better tennis pedigree than Bill. He was the son of Georgia alumnus Larry Shippey, a national senior doubles champion, and the grandson of Georgia Tech alumnus Frank (Hop) Owens, Southern Men's champion in 1922.

Bill's dad started him off at a young age, and Bill was state champion in all the junior age groups. He and Richard Howell were the best "little boys" doubles team I ever saw, and how they could lob! They played together at least 10 years and were one of the best state men's doubles teams I ever saw, too.

I was overjoyed when Bill entered Georgia in September 1965. Frosh weren't eligible for the varsity at that time, but they had their own division in the conference tournament. Bill won the singles, upsetting heavily favored Armistead Neely of Florida in the semis and then nipping Tennessee's Tommy Mozur in the finals.

Bill was one of the most valuable — and unsung — players in Georgia history. He helped us develop the crucial foundation that has enabled us to dominate Southeastern Conference tennis the past 25 years. He made All-SEC all three of his varsity years, playing No. 1 singles for us in '67 and '68 and No. 2 (behind All-American Danny Birchmore) in '69. He also played No. 1 doubles for us all three years, and he was even better in doubles than he was in singles.

Stalwarts from '69 include (l-r) Brant Bailey, Bill Shippey, Norman Holmes and Danny Birchmore.

I think the best match he ever played for us was against Florida's great All-American Charley Owens in the finals of the 1969 SEC No. 2 singles. Owens won a cliffhanger, 11-9, 6-4, and the SEC coaches agreed it was one of the greatest SEC matches they had ever seen.

As team captain in 1969, Bill almost led us to our first SEC team title, but Florida's greatest team ever (led by Neely, Owens, Jamie Pressley and Steve Beeland) was too tough.

Since graduation Bill has become one of the best in the business of building and resurfacing tennis courts. He resurfaces his alma mater's courts every other year so they'll be "Shippey-shape" (sorry) for the NCAAs.

By the way, I've had several coaches (after we've beaten

their teams in the NCAA) accuse me of having Bill make our courts slow, thus giving our backcourt players a better chance to win. Completely untrue. I even complained to Bill myself one year during Mikael Penfors' championship run. I told Bill that Mikael was too impatient to play long points, that he liked faster courts and wanted to be able to hit winners from the backcourt.

But Bill answered, "You know you asked me to make the courts the best speed for an all-court game — not too fast, not too slow, but *just right*. And I'm sure you remember when Tut Bartzen [TCU's Hall of Fame coach] told you that Georgia's courts were the best speed for all-court play he had ever seen."

Bill was absolutely right, as usual.

Doubles: The Thinking Game

Although I knew next to nothing about doubles when I began coaching collegiate tennis, I gradually learned to love it and enjoyed coaching doubles as much as anything I ever did in tennis. I'm sure that several of my old friends would turn over in their graves if they knew that some of my doubles teams had won major victories while carrying out my instructions.

The first such friend would be my old basketball coach and chemistry professor at Athens High, Mr. Sam Gardner, who introduced me to the game of doubles. When I was a sophomore in high school (1936), Mr. Gardner asked me to play doubles with Earl Berry (the state high school singles champion) in the district qualifying tournament for the Georgia High School State Championships. I told Mr. Gardner that I had played few tennis singles matches and had *never* played a game of doubles. "Well," he said, "you're the state ping-pong champion in both singles and doubles, and I believe you can catch on to tennis doubles right away."

But Mr. Gardner, a good basketball coach who didn't know much about tennis, was wrong. We did win the district tournament because of Earl Berry's stellar play and also because the other "country boys" in the tournament didn't know any more about tennis than I did. But we bowed out quickly in the state tournament because our opponents were smart enough to direct most of their shots at me.

Twenty years later, when I became Georgia's tennis coach in 1955, I still didn't know much about doubles. But because I was eager to learn the doubles game, in my second season as Georgia coach I invited Malon Courts (one of Georgia's greatest players, whose son Richard was on our team) to sit with me at our match with Georgia Tech in Atlanta. I especially wanted Malon to give me some doubles pointers. He was one of the nation's best senior doubles players, having won the USTA 45 doubles with his friend, the brilliant Bitsy Grant.

After observing our doubles play, Malon said we were too defensive minded. He didn't like both of our men playing on the baseline when the other team was serving. He wanted the non-receiving player at the net. And, for more aggressive play, he suggested the receiver (when possible) follow his return to the net, joining his partner — always striving to control the net play.

However, our players were not nearly as skilled as Malon was in employing those tactics. Our boys were strictly back-court, clay-court players who could drive and lob the ball pretty well, but they were not adept at chipping the return and following it to the net and they were also weak volleyers.

Malon proceeded to show me some good drills designed to improve the chip return and the volleying game, and from that day onward I have spent considerable time in the study of winning doubles. It has been a fascinating pursuit. Doubles is a much more scientific and complex game than singles — which, of course, is why I have enjoyed coaching it so much.

When you think about it, you realize that college and high

school coaches usually don't get players who have had a great deal of training in doubles. Their players may have received singles coaching from teaching pros, but it is usually up to the high school and college coaches to *make* doubles players out of their material.

Another reason I so thoroughly enjoyed coaching doubles — besides the fact that it is so scientific — was that we usually ended our long daily practice sessions with several sets of doubles, and it was relaxing and fun compared to the hard work in drills and singles sets that comprised the earlier part of our daily routine.

Our practices usually began with close to an hour of drills, at full speed, no loafing allowed — followed by two sets of singles or an 8-game pro set under match conditions. Then we'd have a break, at which time I would critique each man on his play. Finally came the fun part: after pairing our four doubles teams, I would privately talk to each one of them, advising the tactics to use against their foe of the day. Then I would sit in my favorite corner of the bleachers, yelling "great play" if warranted but just as often yelling "that's not the way to do it" or "that won't win."

I was rather conservative in my doubles coaching, an adherent of "book doubles" or "disciplined doubles," as I preferred to term it. I wanted the fundamentals mastered, nothing fancy — just like blocking and tackling in football.

The main things we emphasized for the serving team were:

- get the first serve in to the opponent's weak side most of the time, but vary it for surprise, especially with deep serves straight into the body;
- get to the net fast every time;
- play your half of the court but decide in advance which player will take the drives or lobs down the

middle of the court, and get out of the way when your partner yells, "I got it";

■ never guess on poaches but be ready to hop on a floater;

■ use the Australian system if an opponent is killing your serve with winning returns (that is, your partner will occupy the same side of the net from which you're serving, to defend against the cross-court return, and you will hustle fast to cover the alley he has left open).

I also emphasized that you don't have to win with the first volley, but you certainly do have to get it back in play, preferably deep unless you have a set-up that can be put away. I preached that points are generally won with superior net position and net control; you need to be careful with the overhead smash (don't "Big Ike" 'em), and you have to be patient against good, high and deep lobs, letting 'em bounce if necessary.

Serving teams are broken less often by good shots by the receiving team than by the serving team's own errors: a double fault, a volley or overhead error, or some fancy shot going astray when another shot should have been attempted.

On the receiving team, I emphasized:

■ you must get the serve back in play;

■ be willing to make a defensive shot against the harder first serve, the bread-and-butter first service return being aimed low down the middle or, if the receiver notices the net man planning to poach, then lob over him;

■ vary the returns with occasional drives down the alley to keep the net man honest;

■ assuming you've mastered the shot, follow Malon Courts' strategy of chipping the return and

following into net position;
- blast a short serve straight at the net man.

I also preferred our receiving team to play back on the first serve, concentrating on getting the return safely in play and then being ready, if possible, to attack the ensuing volley or to lob if both opponents had commanding net position.

The receiving team should prearrange which player will take the volleys down the center of the court. Usually, I assigned the player with the stronger or more reliable stroke.

Most college players I have coached in doubles were too impatient when freshman — too anxious to win the point with their first shot. I tried to teach them to be patient, hit the right shot and wait for the opening.

A coach can form a winning doubles team very easily if both his players have "big" serves that are hard to break, but he also can have a championship defensive team — like Danny Birchmore and Norman Holmes, SEC No. 1 doubles champions in 1971. The best doubles teams, of course, are those that have offensive and defensive strength — like Georgia's NCAA doubles kings in 1983, Allen Miller and Ola Malmqvist.

I also believe that tennis fans, the true aficionados, enjoy watching good doubles matches more than singles battles. The action is faster and the tactics more scientific and subtle.

There are many ways to win in doubles — some of them downright strange.

Bitsy Grant and Bobby Dodd, Georgia Tech's legendary football coach, were a very successful senior doubles team despite the fact that Dodd, as a player, was not in the class of some of the players they beat. Dodd had two good shots — both unorthodox, to say the least, and the tactics Bitsy and Dodd employed to win utilized to the limit their combined talents.

Dodd's two good shots were defensive. When at the net, he volleyed by blocking the ball with a stroke not horizontal or parallel to the court but with his racquet held straight up. And when on the baseline, his best shot was a lob that he executed with a two-handed grip, scooping up the ball directly in front of him. It was known far and wide as the Bobby Dodd Shovel Shot.

Dodd knew that his doubles opponents would try to keep the ball out of Bitsy's reach and would be hitting every possible shot straight at himself. So he would station himself at two strategic spots: either very close to the net on one or the other alley lines, which left almost all of the net for Bitsy to cover; or on one of the corners at the baseline, which left practically the whole court for the fleet-footed Bitsy to handle.

You would be surprised at the number of errors their opponents made trying to hit the ball to Dodd in those corner positions. And of course, they usually tried to hit the ball as hard as they could, the result being that Dodd would simply dodge their shots and the balls would fly out of play. It looked like "dodge ball" instead of tennis.

Incidentally, I tried to employ a similar strategy when I began playing father-son doubles with my son Ham. Actually we won the Southern five times, beginning when Ham was 13 and I was 37. In those days I instructed Ham as follows: when you serve, get off the court as fast as you can and I'll cover the whole court; after receiving serve, get off the court as fast as you can and I'll do the rest. The last time we won the Southern, Ham was playing No. 1 at Princeton. The instructions remained the same, but now Ham was giving them.

And more recently, in 1989, when I had turned 68 years old, I asked Allen Miller (former NCAA doubles champ for Georgia and now pro at the Athens Country Club) if he would help me win the Athens City Open men's doubles. I wanted to win it 50 years after I had first won it at age 18 in 1939.

Always ready for a challenge, Allen agreed to do it, and he carried me all the way. In the finals we won a hard-fought three-setter over fellow Athens pro Nick Stutsman (former Auburn star) and young Corky Warner (local high school champion at Athens Academy and the grandson of former Southern great Bill Umsteadter of LSU), 4-6, 6-2, 6-3. We used pretty much the same tactic that Coach Dodd and Bitsy Grant used so many times to success. That is, I either played one corner of the net with defensive volleys or one corner of the baseline, usually hitting lobs, which left almost the whole court for Allen to handle. And once again, the opposition made tons of errors trying to hit too many hard balls at me — which I would dodge just like Coach Dodd used to do.

When I coached the Southern Junior Davis Cup team in the summer of 1960, my son Ham (a member of the Southern team) hooked up with Mike Belkin of the Florida Sectional team because neither had a partner. They played together three straight weeks, and in their first venture reached the finals of the Louisville (Ky.) Boys' 15 doubles, losing to the national hardcourt champions Gary Rose (later a star at UCLA) and Ian Kucera.

Rose and Kucera were a classical boys' doubles team: good serve-and-volleyers, and they had little trouble with Ham and Mike, who were weak servers and weak volleyers but, nevertheless, attempted to play the conventional serve-and-volley doubles game. The hard-hitting Californians won easily, 6-2, 6-2.

After the match, in our station wagon on the way to the next tournament at Springfield, Ohio (the Western Boys), Mike rode with us because we had more room than the

Florida team did in its car. We discussed the Louisville match at length. Mike and Ham both said they hoped they got a chance to play the Californians in the Westerns because they knew they'd beat them the next time. I replied that they had absolutely no chance of getting revenge unless they played the entire match from the back court.

"You boys are the two best backcourt, clay-court players in the country in your age group," I told them. "You have strong ground strokes and good lobs. You lost at Louisville because you came to the net on weak serves that they knocked down your throats, and furthermore your volleys were pitiful. If you stay back throughout the match, you might beat Rose and Kucera if you get another chance."

Well, guess what? The same teams met again in the finals at Springfield with Ham and Mike carrying out their new battle plan to perfection. They won by the same scores they had lost at Louisville — 6-2, 6-2 — driving the Californians crazy with their great defensive backcourt game of lobs mixed with timely drives.

Our boys were so impressive at Springfield that they were seeded No. 1 in the nationals at Kalamazoo the next week. Kalamazoo in those days had slow red clay courts, and I believe Ham and Mike might have won there, too. But it had rained for several days, forcing their quarterfinal match onto fast hard courts which favored their opponents — a very good serve-and-volley team of Mickey Schad (later a star at Miami) and Nick Kalo (later a Greek Davis Cupper). Schad and Kalo won a close match — and went on to capture the title.

Mike and Ham went on to outstanding singles records, especially Belkin, who won the USTA Boys' 15 and 18 singles, reached the finals of the 1965 NCAAs (representing Miami) and starred several years for the Canadian Davis Cup team (he was born in Canada but grew up in Miami Beach, Fla.).

But the highlight of their doubles careers definitely was at Springfield, Ohio, in the summer of 1960 when they played every shot from the backcourt to upset the national hard-court boys' champions.

In the 1971 NCAAs at Notre Dame I had a superb defensive doubles team of Danny Birchmore and Norman Holmes. They had won the SEC No. 1 division, also the fast Princeton Indoors and were 25-1 going into the NCAAs, having lost only to North Carolina's outstanding Freddie McNair and Richard McKee (NCAA finalists two years later).

Danny and Norman used somewhat the same tactics as my son Ham and Mike Belkin did in their boys' 15 doubles successes 11 years earlier. That is, they won with mostly back-court defensive play: good drives and good lobs. They could run down almost all overhead smashes or short angle volleys. Unlike Ham and Mike, they did take the net on their serves, which were pretty good. Norman had a fine topspin serve and Danny had a reliable, accurate slice and topspin. Their volleys were not severe, but they seldom erred on volleys and could place them on a dime.

It was a hugh draw of 128 teams in the doubles at Notre Dame in 1971. Danny and Norman were seeded 9-16 and won three matches in a row in straight sets to reach the round of 16. Here they faced the No. 3 seeds, Marcelo Lara (a Mexican Davis Cup star) and Dick Bohrnstedt of Southern California. The Trojans had never seen so many lobs thrown up at them, and they consequently lost patience; they tried to smash too many overheads too hard and ended up making a lot of errors. We won, 6-3, 6-3.

In the quarters, however, Coach Glenn Bassett of UCLA must have instructed his fine team of Jimmy Connors (later a Wimbledon doubles champion as well as singles) and Jeff Austin (brother of U.S. Open women's champion Tracy

Austin) to be patient on our lobs. Connors and Austin were too good, 6-2, 6-4.

But our team's fine showing was further proof that winning doubles is not just about power; it's about planning the best strategy to use the strokes you've got.

An interesting thing about the great game of doubles is that the Americans — ex-collegians in particular — continue to garner more Grand Slam titles than players from other countries. Just check the statistics of the past 16 years: former U.S. collegiate players have won 31 of the 60 Grand Slam doubles diadems. Australians have collected the second most — 17 — and Sweden is third with nine. And it doesn't matter whether the matches are played on grass, clay or hard-surfaced courts. We win most of the time. The U.S. collegians have annexed the Australian Open eight of 15 years (it was not held in 1986); the French Open six of 15; Wimbledon seven of 15; and the U.S. Open 10 of 15.

A major reason for the U.S. dominance in doubles, I think, is due to the special emphasis placed on doubles in collegiate competition in the United States. (I was glad to hear Mary Carillo of ESPN express this same opinion chatting with Cliff Drysdale and Fred Stolle during the 1994 U.S.-Netherlands Davis Cup tie.) In the unique collegiate dual-match format, which calls for both singles and doubles play to determine the overall winner, a team must excel in both. Therefore, American college coaches have their players practice doubles about as much as they do singles. In other countries, on the other hand, where collegiate tennis is practically non-existent, the teaching pros spend little time on the finer points of doubles.

Australia's comparative success in doubles play is due to two reasons. First, the most important part of doubles is the serve-and-volley game, and Australians, who play more on grass than other players do, must master the serve-and-volley to do well on grass. Second, Australians always have taken great pride in Davis Cup play, where the doubles point is often decisive, so their Davis Cup coaches through the years (particularly the peerless Harry Hopman) have emphasized doubles play.

Incidentally, college players have accounted for all 31 American Grand Slam doubles crowns since 1980; but the collegians won only half of the 22 Grand Slam singles titles during this same period: non-collegians Jim Courier, Pete Sampras, Andre Agassi, and Michael Chang have won the other eleven.

U.S. college tennis rightfully is proud of its players who have excelled in professional doubles play, and special recognition should be given the college coaches whose protégés have won numerous Grand Slam doubles titles and also won the crucial doubles point many times in U.S. Davis Cup battles.

George Toley's Southern California players went on to win 16 Grand Slam doubles titles. In fact, two of his doubles teams — both NCAA champions — are considered among the best in the annals of tennis: Dennis Ralston and Rafael Osuna, the Mexican wizard, and Stan Smith and Bob Lutz.

Protégés of Dick Gould at Stanford also have captured 17 Grand Slam men's doubles titles. His most famous player, John McEnroe, often has been acclaimed as the most brilliant doubles player of modern times.

Glenn Bassett of UCLA also turned out many great doubles players, and his boys went on to capture 14 Grand Slam crowns. Ex-Bruin Peter Fleming was Coach Bassett's most successful doubles product, joining McEnroe for numerous Wimbledon, U.S. Open, and U.S. Davis Cup victories.

Dick Leach, Coach Toley's successor at Southern Cal, has developed players good enough to win six Grand Slam doubles events in recent years, and they are still young enough to win more. His son Rick has won four Grand Slam titles: the Australian twice, Wimbledon and the U.S. Open.

Here's a complete run-down of American ex-collegians who have won Grand Slam doubles titles since 1980:

Australian: 1984, Sherwood Stewart (Lamar College) and non-collegian Mark Edmondson of Australia; 1985, Paul Annacone (Tennessee) and Christo Van Rensburg of South Africa; 1988–89, Rick Leach (USC) and Jim Pugh (UCLA); 1990, Pieter Aldrich (Miami) and Danie Visser of South Africa; 1991, Scott Davis (Stanford) and David Pate (TCU); 1994, Paul Haarhuis (Armstrong State and Florida State) and Jacco Eltingh of the Netherlands; 1995, Richey Reneberg (SMU) and Jared Palmer (Stanford).

French: 1980, Victor Amaya (Michigan) and Hank Pfister (San Jose State); 1982, Sherwood Stewart (Lamar State) and Ferdi Taygan (UCLA); 1987, Robert Seguso (SIU-Edwardsville) and Anders Jarryd of Sweden; 1989, Patrick McEnroe (Stanford) and Jim Grabb (Stanford); 1993, Luke Jensen (USC) and Murphy Jensen (Georgia); 1994, Jonathan Stark (Stanford) and Byron Black (USC).

Wimbledon: 1981, '83, and '84, John McEnroe (Stanford) and Peter Fleming (Michigan and UCLA); 1987–88, Ken Flach (SIU-Edwardsville) and Robert Seguso (SIU-Edwardsville); 1990, Rick Leach (USC) and Jim Pugh (UCLA); 1992, John McEnroe (Stanford) and Michael Stitch of Germany.

U.S.: 1980, Bob Lutz (USC) and Stan Smith (USC); 1982, Kevin Curren (Texas) and Steve Denton (Texas); 1981 and '83, John McEnroe (Stanford) and Peter Fleming (Michigan and UCLA); 1985, Ken Flach (SIU-Edwardsville) and Robert Seguso (SIU-Edwardsville); 1983, John McEnroe (Stanford) and Mark Woodforde of Australia; 1990, Pieter Aldrich (Miami) and Danie Visser of South Africa; 1992, Jim Grabb (Stanford) and Richey Reneberg (SMU); 1993, Ken Flach (SIU-Edwardsville) and Rick Leach (USC); 1994, Paul Haarhuis (Armstrong State and Florida State) and Jacco Eltingh of the Netherlands.

CHAPTER 3

A Short Essay on Percentage Tennis

"Percentage tennis" simply means attempting the right shot every time, which is determined by both your own position on the court and your opponent's position. Percentage tennis means playing smart tennis. The top players and most experienced players seldom attempt the wrong shot, the so-called low-percentage shot.

The best illustration of the low-percentage shot I've ever seen comes from one of my early teams. On that team I had a boy, a good player, who hit more balls just slightly deep or wide than any player I ever saw. One day I said to him: "Chuck, you ought to have more margin of error. You're hitting too many balls out by just an inch or two." He replied, "But, Coach, I'm aiming for the lines. I thought that's what you are supposed to do." I replied, "Hell, no. You're not supposed to aim for the lines; you're supposed to aim at least a yard from the line unless it's a passing shot or serve."

But I will say this about Chuck. While he hit a lot of balls out by inches, he also hit more lines than any player we ever had.

The most common "dumb" shot hit by young players and

even many collegiate players is the drive when a lob is called for. When your opponent has good net position and you are deep in the court, the percentage shot is the lob. That sounds very simple, but you would be surprised how many players will still try to drive the ball through an opponent with commanding net position, and they lose the point almost every time.

When your opponent at the net has both your line return and crosscourt return well covered, and you are deep in the court, you *must* lob. And your goal with the lob is to push your opponent off his commanding net position. You should attempt to get the ball completely over his head so that it lands behind him, or at least push him back to a depth in the court (well past the service line) that will reduce his chances of hitting an effective overhead.

If you keep your eye on your opponent all the time, you should know where to hit your shot every time. If he lingers in the corner, drive the ball to the opposite corner and keep him on the run. If you drive the ball with pace, corner to corner, sooner or later your opponent will hit you a short ball or make an error.

One of your constant goals is to get depth on your shots, whether you're playing a baseliner or net rusher. It's tough for a net rusher to get commanding net position if you can keep the ball deep into his court.

Another popular low-percentage shot is the over-hit service return, especially off your opponent's first serve. Be defensive-minded on most first service returns. Aim low down the middle of the net. Your best bet to win a point against a strong server is to run down his first volley and then make the percentage shot: the down-the-line or crosscourt passing shot or the lob.

Remember that it is not always necessary to make clean passing shots to win the point. Simply "stretch" your opponent to the alley, pulling him out of position so that you have a big hole to drive through on your next shot.

Be patient. You should be in a hurry to get to the ball but not in a hurry to win the point. Work it up. Maneuver your opponent out of position just as a boxer sets up his foe for a knockout blow.

You give yourself a tremendous advantage when you learn to disguise your shots effectively. When your opponent has commanding net position, make him think you're going to drive the ball to a certain spot; then at the very last moment lob the ball over his head. Or do just the reverse: fake the lob and then drive the ball.

There are two positions on the court you must learn to play: the baseline and the net.

First, you must understand that a tennis court is a huge area for one person to cover. A centerfielder in baseball or safetyman in football has a lot of ground to cover, but he might play a whole game without a single ball being hit or thrown to his territory. Not so in the game of tennis singles, in which the player constantly must run up and down the court and from one corner to the other.

Good baseline position is in the center of the court, a foot or two behind the baseline. Some players prefer to play closer to the baseline than others, especially those who want to rush the net at the first chance. Naturally, if your opponent hits many deep topspin drives, he will keep you well back of the baseline.

If you are in poor baseline position (for instance, playing inside the baseline), you will have difficulty handling a hard-hit deep ball. Keep in mind that it is much more difficult to move backwards to get in the proper position to stroke the ball than it is to move forward for a shot.

When you move to the corner of the court to hit a shot, you must immediately return to good baseline position: the center of the court. The most common error in position play is lingering in the corner after hitting the ball and thus giving your opponent the opportunity to drive the ball to the opposite corner. Once your opponent gets you on the run, he'll generally win the point.

But remember: tennis is a running game. You must be ready to run all the time, hustle all the time — concentrate, think and compete all the time. Your opponent probably will do the same thing. Somebody will lose. It's only disgraceful to fail to do your best. If you have to go down, go down fighting.

It's relatively easy to play good baseline position if you hustle and keep your eye on the ball. When you are in good baseline position, it usually takes only one or two steps to get to the ball. And a player who gets to the ball in good time ought to be able to hit it pretty close to his target every time.

You'll often be pulled out of good baseline position by a ball that bounces short. When handling a short ball, you must decide whether to take the net on an approach shot or hit the ball deep and return to the baseline. The general rule is to take the shorter route — whether it's on up to the net or back to the baseline.

There are two net positions: first, if you approach down the center of the court, you should stand at the center of the net, anywhere from three to six feet from it (a shorter person definitely should not get too close to the net because it's easy for his opponent to lob over him); second, if you hit the approach to a corner of the court, you should take a net position in the center of that side of the court, being sure you can cover the down-the-line passing shot and the crosscourt shot that will clear the net roughly at its center.

Remember! It's dangerous to hit a crosscourt approach because it is difficult to reach the passing shot down the alley line farthest from you. On the other hand, it's not bad tactics to approach crosscourt if you have your opponent on the run or if you know you're hitting to your opponent's weak side.

When receiving serve, you should stand in the corner in a position that will enable you to reach a crosscourt slice to the alley line, and also be ready to step quickly toward the ball if it is hit down the center stripe.

Let's simply concede that a good server has a big advantage on the receiver. He is capable of overpowering you, and you probably won't break him often. Your best bet is to strive hard to get his serve back in play and hope he makes some errors on his volley or overhead. Strong servers usually are not broken by your good play; they usually are broken when they double fault, make a couple of errors, and you happen to make one good shot.

Bide your time against a strong server. Hope he misses the first one. There are not many players whose second serve is so strong that you cannot make a decent return on it.

(Note: When facing a lefthanded server, stand a foot or two more to the left because the lefthander's slice or topspin serve normally will break to your left.)

If you are involved in a baseline battle, remember that you must be prepared to outhustle, outfight, outtough your opponent in the long rallies. Steadfast resolve helps win the long baseline rallies. Say to yourself, "I'm just as tough and as determined as my opponent; I can hit as many balls back over the net as he can."

Good footwork and racquet preparation are necessary to make consistently strong shots. You can make a better shot if you are in perfect position for your stroke, the same as a baseball batter who waits for the ball to cross the plate where he likes it best. Of course, some gifted athletes are so agile and acrobatic that they can hit a ball off-balance. That's one of the reasons they become champions.

An instructor can teach you the proper footwork, proper racquet preparation and proper stroke technique. How good you get to be depends on how hard you practice, your desire and how much athletic ability and aptitude you possess.

But all champions must play percentage tennis, and they are rarely caught out of good position on the court.

CHAPTER 4

Characters
on the Court

LARRY SHIPPEY,
WORLD-CLASS PRANKSTER

Every tennis center has at least one court jester among its "regulars," and one of the best is University of Georgia alumnus Larry Shippey at Atlanta's famed Bitsy Grant Tennis Center. For years, Larry has hung around the Grant Center with some of the best senior players who ever played the game: Tom Bird, Hank Crawford, Coach Bobby Dodd, Dr. Glen Dudley, Vince Connerat, Red Enloe, Prof. G. A. York and the great Bitsy himself. In addition to being an outstanding player, Larry is a champion prankster, and few of his victims ever knew Larry was the perpetrator.

I was a good friend of Larry's, even though he was a few years older than I. I had known him when he came up from Waycross, Ga., and was a student at Georgia in the mid-1930s, living at the Athens YMCA. We used to play a lot of ping-pong. And years later I was overjoyed when his son Bill, the state junior champion, accepted the first tennis scholarship in Georgia's history.

All this friendship notwithstanding, Larry made me a victim of one of his best jokes during a Georgia State tournament in the 1950s. I happened to be playing an Atlanta doctor in the first round and was playing on Court 1, right in front of the Grant Center's main grandstand. Early in the match, I hit a first serve that I thought was smack on the line, but my opponent yelled, "Out." Then my second serve hit squarely in the middle of the service box, but my opponent again called, "Out."

I bounded up to the net and asked, "What's going on here? My second serve was good by several feet."

"It was just as out as the ball I hit a few shots ago that you called out," declared my opponent. He was referring to a call I had made on a drive of his that had landed a few inches beyond the baseline.

Then I noticed a lot of giggling going on in the grandstand amongst a group that included head pro Jack Rodgers (later Georgia Tech's coach), Bitsy Grant, Tom Bird and Larry Shippey. When I noticed Shippey laughing, I knew that something was fishy and that some kind of joke was being played on me. But I was mad at the doctor, who was not a strong player, and from that point on I played every ball he hit that landed on my side of the court, even if it was out a foot or more.

Once, the doctor questioned an "out" ball that he had hit, and I replied, "I'll call the shots on my side of the court; you just call 'em on your side."

Of course, all this greatly amused my "friends" in the grandstand, and before long a goodly crowd of fans had gathered to see the feud going on. I won the match, 6-0, 6-0, but it was closer than the score. I had to run almost to Jericho chasing down all his "out" shots.

Later, I learned that Rodgers and Shippey had masterminded this prank. They had told the good doctor, who was notorious for being hotheaded and paranoid about opponents' calls, that I was the worst cheater in the game and that he should challenge any close call I made.

Larry Shippey not only is a great joke-puller, he also is a fine joke-teller, and one of his best is on himself, which I have heard him tell on countless occasions.

It was in the USTA National 45 Grass Court doubles championships. Larry and Bitsy Grant, who had won the USTA 45 Clay Court doubles a record six times together, were trying to topple the great international pair of Jean Borotra and Adrian Quist at old Forest Hills in front of a large crowd.

The umpire was in rare form, making the introductions in a most pompous manner:

"To my right, six times a member of the victorious French Davis Cup team, winner of five Grand Slam singles titles and 10 doubles diadems at Wimbledon, the French and the Australian championships, one of the greatest players of all time, Jean Borotra of France.

"And his equally illustrious partner, winner of three Grand Slam singles titles and 13 Grand Slam doubles diadems, mainstay of 12 Australian Davis Cup teams, one of the all-time greats, Adrian Quist of Australia.

"Their opponents, to my left, 11 times Southern Men's Clay Court champion, three times United States National Clay Court champion, six times U.S. National 45 Clay Court champion, undefeated in Davis Cup competition on clay, a mainstay of the victorious 1937 U.S. Davis Cup champions, one of the great clay court players of all time, Bryan M. Grant of the United States.

"And, his partner, Mr. — er — Lawrence Shippey of Atlanta, Ga."

HEIR APPARENT

In 1991 I had the great pleasure of participating in a much-deserved tribute to the co-captain of the University of Georgia's 1965 tennis team, who we all knew at that time would go forth and amount to "something or other." And his legion of friends around the state are delighted that he has proved such a winner in the roughest, toughest game of all, where there are no holds barred, no mercy shown, and no prisoners taken: Georgia (Cracker) politics!

It wasn't surprising to me at all when Pierre Howard, Jr., — I say Junior because I knew his daddy long before I knew him — polled the most votes of any candidate in the 1990 general election, carrying 156 of the state's 159 counties.

In my long association with athletics at the University of Georgia I have never met a brighter boy. Pierre was not only smart, he was even *smart-aleck*.

One time he had the unmitigated gall to challenge my veracity. When he made the University's highest academic society — Phi Beta Kappa — I knew that he would be showing off his precious key to his teammates. So I decided to play a joke on him. I borrowed my wife's Phi Beta Kappa key, and when Pierre showed off his key at practice that afternoon, I sauntered up to him and flashed my wife's key and said, "Why, I do declare, Pierre, your key is the same design as the one I got back in '42."

He was flabbergasted, and stammered, "Why, Coach, I never knew that you made Phi Beta Kappa."

I replied modestly, "It's not a big deal. I just don't make a habit of flaunting it in front of lesser-witted friends."

Pierre's face turned beet-red; I had gotten him good, and I knew he would seek revenge as soon as possible. Having known me for several years, he would have bet his last dollar that I wasn't smart enough to have made Phi Beta Kappa. So he did some checking up, and one day — in front of the whole team — he confronted me in the manner of a criminal lawyer presenting irrefutable evidence.

"Coach Magill, I have found out whose Phi Beta Kappa key you had the other day. I couldn't find your name on the official list of members, but I did notice the maiden name of your wife, Rosemary Reynaud. It was her key — *not yours.*"

Pierre was a regular on our varsity three years and scored many fine victories. As a soph, he was finalist in both the No. 4 singles and No. 2 doubles, helping us to almost upset Tulane for the SEC title. As a junior he and Alex Keller (now an Athens ophthalmologist) won the state collegiate doubles.

Pierre's most memorable match — by far — was during his sophomore year on April 8, 1963, at Tuscaloosa, Ala. Alabama's men's team featured a girl, who happened to be the two-time national collegiate women's champion, Roberta Allison. Furthermore, she was a hometown girl, and whenever she played, she drew a big, partisan crowd that unmercifully razzed her victim of the day.

I was happy that Pierre, of all our players, was matched against Roberta at No. 4 singles because he was more capable of keeping his cool than some of his "rabbit-eared" teammates. Sure enough, the 'Bama fans jumped all over Pierre, hurling such taunts as, "Hey, lard-butt, you're going to get whipped by a girl today!" Pierre labored under these insults throughout the two-hour match under a hot sun, but he prevailed — and even earned a standing ovation when he handed Roberta her first loss of the season, 7-5, 6-2.

One more thing about that match: Pierre was far from a "lard-butt" when the thing was over. He lost 10 pounds in his all-out effort to keep from losing to a girl.

When Pierre threw his hat into the ring for the Lieutenant

Governorship, I told him that his biggest obstacle would be overcoming his name—that Georgia Crackers would distrust anyone with a name like "Pierre." But as might be expected, Pierre adroitly turned his name into an asset by going all over the state and telling people that "Pierre" in French meant "Bubba."

This maneuver received so much publicity throughout the state that the head of Georgia's French Department, Dr. Jean-Pierre Piriou, received several letters in the mail addressed to Dr. Jean-Bubba Piriou. And as fate would have it, Pierre Howard and Pierre Piriou were seated next to each other at a dinner party in Athens that fall. But once again our Pierre saved the moment by conversing with Dr. Piriou in perfect French, and Dr. Piriou was so impressed he is now one of Pierre's staunchest supporters.

TWIN TERRORS IN TENNIS

I've known several sets of twins who played tennis on the University of Georgia courts. Among the earliest were the Manderson twins of Savannah, Ed Jr. and Joe — fine-looking, tall blonds who resembled a young Robert Redford (or two). They were identical twins and played on our freshman team in 1959 when freshmen were not eligible for the varsity. Joe was the better player, actually one of the best doubles players in the country. He possessed a powerful topspin serve, strong volleys and overhead, and an extremely good backhand service return and approach to the net.

I used to kid one of our most loyal supporters, the late Dr. Robert H. West (head of the English Department and president of the Athens Tennis Association) that Joe and Ed Manderson would some day win the SEC No. 1 doubles because I planned to have Joe serve every time and receive every time. I figured that if I couldn't tell them apart, surely their opponents couldn't.

But fate stepped in and thwarted my plans for Joe Manderson to "single-handedly" lead us to the SEC No. 1 doubles title. Ed quit school his freshman year to join the Army and didn't return until brother Joe had graduated. However, Joe almost won the SEC No. 1 doubles his senior year, teaming with the hard-serving Mack Crenshaw.

Incidentally, as freshmen at Georgia, Joe and Ed lived in the attic of the athletic field house (now the Alumni Society's home). I arranged for them to live there free for serving as nightwatchmen.

In the 1980s there appeared in the Crackerland junior tournament two sets of twins in the age 10 group: Jack and Joe Frierson, Jr., of Athens, and Shannan and Shawn McCarthy of Alpharetta. They all became good enough for college scholarships, and three of them came to Georgia. Joe Frierson, Jr., went to North Carolina; but even if he had come to Georgia with brother Jack, I could not have carried out my masterful "Manderson" plan. Jack was left-handed, Joe righthanded, and they weren't identical twins anyway.

But the McCarthy girls were identical twins, and I was quick to share the "Manderson" plan with Georgia women's coach Jeff Wallace, who had been my men's captain in 1984. But Coach Wallace just laughed at my suggestion and didn't even play the twins together much during their four years at UGA. I still believe Shannan and Shawn could have won the NCAA doubles if Coach Wallace had used my strategy. Shannan did almost win the NCAA singles her senior season in 1992, losing a heartbreaker to Lisa Raymond of Florida in the finals after having beaten Raymond twice during the year.

The McCarthy twins: one is Shannon and the other is Shawn.

In the early 1960s I tried to get a friend of mine, former Georgia football and baseball player Marion Gaston (a native of Toccoa, Ga., then living in Burlington, Iowa) to send his twin sons Charley and Joe to Georgia. They had compiled fine junior records in the Midwest. But Joe went to Duke, where he played No. 1, and Charley joined the United States paratroopers. The story goes that his life was miraculously saved on just his second jump. Charley's parachute didn't open, but by the grace of God he was able to grab the traces of a fellow paratrooper whose 'chute had already opened, and they floated safely down to earth together.

When Charley had completed his stint in the service, he did enroll at Georgia, and he played No. 6 as a sophomore, then jumped to No. 1 as a junior in the spring of 1963.

I will never forget perhaps the best match Charley ever played — May 1, 1963, against Georgia Tech in Atlanta. Charley met the Yellow Jackets' ace, George Dickinson, the state's No. 1 collegiate player, in the feature match. Charley had come close to upsetting Dickinson in Athens the previous week, losing a three-setter on our slow clay courts. Now Charley was playing on his favorite surface: hard courts, which he had grown up on in Iowa. Charley won the first set, 8-6, and had triple-match point at 5-6 in the second set with Dickinson serving at love-40. On the first match point, Dickinson double-faulted (no doubt about it), and I thought the match was over. Everybody else did too, and the Georgia supporters proceeded to give Charley a round of applause. But Charley played the double-fault serve, lost the point and the game and the set, 8-6, and then went on to lose the third set, 6-1.

After the match I went up to Charley and said, "Didn't you see that Dickinson double-faulted on your first match point?"

"Yeah, Coach, I knew it," Charley replied, "but I didn't want to win on a double-fault, and I still had two more match points."

I finally realized the real reason Charley played that double-fault on match point was that when he had survived that miraculous parachute descent he must have landed on his head.

Charles now is a successful businessman in Jacksonville, Fla., and I imagine he's probably forgotten about that match. But George Dickinson has never forgotten it. Just last year, at the Georgia State Open Indoors in Athens, George asked me if I remembered that infamous match and commented that Charley was really playing a super match until he had his brainstorm.

George poured some more salt on the old wound by adding, "I believe Georgia Tech won the team match that day, 5-4." To which I added, "What else do you know, George?"

When the 1972 NCAA championships were held at Georgia for the first time in 1972, there were two sets of twins in the field: Tom and Gene Fluri of the University of Missouri, and Tim and Tom Gullikson of little Northern Illinois University. I did about everything myself running off the tournament that year, including handling the P.A. system, and one time I accidentally brought down the house when I announced in my Southern drawl: "Fluri and Fluri of Missouri, report to tournament headquarters." Old coaching friends who were in Athens that year still kid me by asking, "Have you seen Fluri and Fluri of Missouri lately?"

We had a good doubles team that same year in Danny Birchmore and Bob Tanis, but we were knocked off in the first match by the Gullikson twins, Tim and Tom, 7-5, 6-7, 6-2. I was disappointed at losing to those unknowns, but 11 years later those "unknowns" reached the finals at Wimbledon, losing to John McEnroe and Peter Fleming. And Tom Gullikson today coaches the United States Davis Cup team while Tim tutors current world champion Pete Sampras.

By the way, during that tournament I approached the referee, the incomparable Mike Blanchard, and said, "Mike, be sure to have your umpires closely watch those sets of twins, the Fluris and Gulliksons. The better player might serve every time and receive every time. I once knew an unscrupulous coach in our league capable of doing that with twins on his team."

Mike thought I was kidding, but he did instruct his umpires to watch out for any skullduggery.

THE AGENT FROM HELL

I had great fun helping induct the peerless Richard Howell into the Georgia State Tennis Hall of Fame in 1993. Among the members present on that occasion was Bitsy Grant, the state's greatest player ever, and I pointed out that Richard and Bitsy shared something in common.

Bitsy's father, B. M. Grant, Sr., and his partner Nat Thornton were the first Southerners to reach the finals of the U.S. National championships. They did it in 1907 at The Casino in Newport, losing to the four-time national champions Fred Alexander of Princeton and Harold Hackett of Yale. Mr. Grant spent a lot of time teaching tennis to Bitsy's older brother Berrien, but, according to Bitsy, his father wouldn't help him because he thought Bitsy was too small to become a good player. So Bitsy's mother was the one who taught him how to play, and Bitsy always explained how he became a better player than brother Berrien by saying, "Mother was a better teacher that Dad."

Like Bitsy Grant, Richard Howell also was taught how to play tennis by his mother, Carrie, and Carrie Howell is probably the best "mother" tennis teacher in the history of the state. Her four sons — Arthur Jr. (better known as Speed), Richard, Peter, and Jimbo, along with daughters Eleanor and Lindy — all were good tournament players.

I first became acquainted with the distinguished Howell family while playing in the Atlanta City and Georgia State tournaments back in the 1950s and '60s. My son Ham and I for years played the Howells, Arthur Sr. and Speed, in father-son doubles tournaments. I was pleased to see Speed later excel at his father's alma mater Princeton University. In fact, Speed played on the famous Princeton team that snapped Miami's national collegiate dual match consecutive victory streak at 137 in 1964 — in Coral Gables, too.

Ham was older than Richard, but they played each other in junior tournaments and became friends. Carrie would invite Ham to stay with Richard when in Atlanta for tournaments, and we, in turn, had Richard stay with us when he came to the Crackerland.

I recall Ham's telling me about the time he and Richard played Carrie and a friend of hers in doubles on the Howells' private court; Richard kept telling Ham, "Hit it to Mother's backhand. She's blind as a bat in her right eye."

I vividly remember Richard sitting on our sofa in his tennis attire with his legs dangling (too short to reach the floor), always with two sweat bands on each arm when he was too young to sweat, and constantly spouting the batting averages and pitching records of all the major league stars, past and present. He would even follow my wife Rosemary and our housekeeper Gertrude around the house reciting the latest stats on Willie Mays and Hank Aaron — as if they cared.

Richard and Bill Shippey probably won more state doubles titles, counting boys' 12, 14, 16, 18 and men's divisions, than any other team in state history. They were a fantastic defensive team — world class lobbers. Recently I asked Bill what he thought was the strongest part of Richard's game.

"Richard's greatest talent in tennis by far," Bill answered with no hesitation, "was his uncanny knack of always picking the best possible player as his doubles partner. He started out with me, but we lost in the finals of the USTA Boys' 12 doubles. So he immediately ditched me and latched onto Zan Guerry, and they won the boys' 14 doubles the very next year. Then he ditched Zan for Ham Magill, and I will never forget how they beat Thomas Benedict and me for the state boys' doubles title at Bitsy Grant Center.

Richard Howell (l), before evolving into the agent from hell, enjoys a Coke with Henry Feild.

"On a crucial point, late in the third set, Richard hit a ball that was going a mile out, and Thomas reached up and caught it before it hit the fence.

"Richard went running over to umpire Carleton Fuller and yelled, 'That's our point. The rules say you can't catch the ball before it hits the ground. Ain't that right, Mr. Umpire?'

"The umpire upheld Richard. And that's the way it has been all his life: he always has the facts, and he knows the law."

As would be expected, Richard had a distinguished record at Westminster Prep and at Princeton University, where he won the first annual Princeton Indoor doubles in 1970. Once again he had the best player in the East as his partner — Big Bill Colson. They beat Georgia's Danny Birchmore and Norman Holmes in the finals. I couldn't go up for the tournament and sent my graduate student assistant coach, none other than Bill Shippey. You can imagine what a bitter pill it was for Bill to have his team lose to his lifelong "friend" Richard.

Following graduation at Princeton, Richard made another smart move. He came to the University of Georgia Law School, from which he graduated in 1974. He practiced law 10 years in Atlanta; then he did what he was "born to do." He formed Robinson-Humphrey Sports Enterprises in 1985, and one of his first clients was Georgia's great tennis player Mikael Pernfors.

It was my pleasure to be with Richard in Paris in 1986 when Mikael had his greatest hour in the French Open, knocking off Edberg, Becker, and LeConte on the way to the finals against Ivan Lendl in his prime.

I'll never forget how sick Richard looked when Mikael lost the first set to Becker, 6-0, in the quarters. Just that morning Richard had negotiated a fat contract with Nike, and he didn't relish the prospect of Becker's humiliating Mikael. Fortunately, Mikael turned the match around and won the next three sets, and suddenly Richard had a hot commodity.

When Richard was finalizing his contract with Georgia's great running back Garrison Hearst, he told Garrison that he had always been a staunch Georgia football fan. But I well recall that he grew up a diehard Tech fan and that he could scarcely bring himself to congratulate me when Georgia won the annual Tech-Georgia game. Of course, agents are paid to know the right thing to say.

Even if Richard goes on to become the first agent for a president of the United States (and I would not be surprised if he did), I can tell you right now what will be engraved on his tombstone: the immortal epithet hung on him by Jerry Jones and Jimmy Johnson, the owner and the coach of the world champion Dallas Cowboys, after Richard had negotiated Emmett Smith's monstrous, multimillion dollar contract:

RICHARD UPDYKE SHERMAN HOWELL
"The Agent from Hell"

"WOLLEY, WOLLEY, WOLLEY"

One of my most unforgettable players at Georgia was a little lefthander from Madras, India: Elango Ranganathan. He was blessed with a wonderful sense of humor, and he spoke English better than any of our American players with that clipped British accent like all his fellow countrymen who speak English.

When Elango was only 15 years old, he came to Anderson (S.C.) Junior College where he played No. 2 on the team his freshman year in 1974 and No. 1 in 1975. My first glimpse of Elango came in April 1974 when his Anderson team played our junior varsity in Athens. He lost a close match to Georgia's Andy Homeyer, but he impressed me very much as having the potential to be a fine player. After the match when Elango asked me if I thought he was good enough to get a scholarship to Georgia, I told him there was a good chance and for him to keep in touch with me. Sure enough, I awarded him a scholarship, and he entered Georgia in September 1975. But since he was so young (only 16) and since we also had a veteran team on hand, I held him out of competition to give him more training.

After his first quarter of school Elango went home to Madras where he captured the Indian Boys' 18 national championship in December. When he returned to Athens he brought me a gift: a stuffed mongoose fighting its mortal enemy, the king cobra (wrapped around the mongoose with its hooded head poised to strike). It was so lifelike that it scared the living daylights out of me when I first saw it — just as it startled everyone else who saw it in my office. And for years my children took it to school for "show and tell," where it was always a big hit.

Elango was a standout player at Georgia, being runner-up in the SEC No. 5 singles in both 1977 and 1978, and he helped us win the SEC team titles those years, too.

I'll never forget Elango's great play that helped us win the conference team title in Gainesville, Fla., in May 1977. The tournament shaped up as a toss-up between defending co-champions LSU and Alabama, Georgia and host Florida. There was bad blood between the partisan Florida fans and the Georgia players because of an incident that had occurred during the dual match at Gainesville earlier that season. Georgia had managed to win that match, 5-4; but the hostile Gator crowd had intimidated several Georgia players, particularly the mild-mannered, peace-loving Elango, who was so rattled by catcalls that he and Tim Delaney lost their only SEC doubles match of the season to the Gators' No. 3 team of Charles Wadlington and Bill Tompkins.

A month later the Georgia players returned to Gainesville

Elango Ranganathan

with revenge on their minds and a fierce determination to win the SEC title in front of the Gator Intimidators. On the last day of the tournament the stage was set. When I went to the motel to pick up Elango and Tim for their doubles finals match against none other than the same Wadlington and

Tompkins of Florida, I told Elango and Tim that they could clinch the team championship for Georgia by avenging their previous loss to the Gator pair. I emphasized that they would damn-sure have to disregard the catcalls certain to come from the Gator fans.

I knew Delaney, a fierce competitor who thrived on chips-down situations, would be at his best for this match, but I was not sure about mild-mannered Elango, who definitely had been thrown off his game by the home crowd in the previous match. After seeing the resolute look on Elango's face, though, I knew he was ready to play the match of his life, especially when he said to me in his native dialect, "Don't worry, Coach. I'm going out there and wolley, wolley, wolley!"

I understood him well enough, and was happy as he and Tim were when they defeated Tompkins and Wadlington in straight sets, 7-5, 6-1, completely putting the quietus on the Gator Intimidators in that final set.

A BRUSH WITH ROYALTY

My very first foreign player was a short, pudgy Iraqi from Baghdad by the name of Zuhair Nejib. He came to Georgia to study agriculture and was not a recruited player. (We didn't have any scholarships in his day, anyway.) But he was a pretty good player and won most of his matches at singles positions 4, 5 and 6 during his two-year stint on the varsity. Above all, he was a gentleman and had a keen sense of humor, too.

Zuhair seemed to be very proud of having played on Georgia's team, and he often asked me to send him Georgia Bulldog decals to stick on his car back in Baghdad.

A fellow Iraqi Georgia student once told me that Zuhair

Zuhair Nejib, royalty.

was a descendent of the great Babylonian king, Nebuchadnezzar (Iraq now occupies the land formerly known as Babylon). I certainly didn't doubt it because Zuhair was clearly "too royal" to drag our old clay tennis courts. In his day I had our players drag and roll the courts following practice each day, but early on Zuhair balked at this menial task.

"Coach," he told me, "in my country members of my family never do this type of work."

I replied, "Zuhair, you are in the United States of America now, a democracy, and this type of work is not demeaning to us. I'll tell you what I will do: I'll drag half the court, and you drag the other half."

He agreed, reluctantly — no doubt praying to Allah not to let King Nebuchadnezzar learn of his disgrace.

I was very fond of Zuhair, and during the Persian Gulf War, when our armed forces were "whipping up" on Saddam Hussein and his men, I was worried about Zuhair's safety. My lettermen's letters to him during the war had been returned with big red letters stamped on them: POSTAL SERVICE TEMPORARILY SUSPENDED. However, after the war, they were not returned, and I was greatly relieved to once again receive his annual Christmas card.

Familiar Names

BITSY GRANT

When I was a boy learning to play tennis in the mid-1930s, Bitsy Grant was my idol. I would catch the bus from Athens to Atlanta to watch him play matches, and later I even took the train to New York City to see him in the U.S. Championships at Forest Hills. After World War II, when I was tennis editor, among other duties, with the *Atlanta Journal*, it was my pleasure finally to meet Bitsy and begin a friendship with him that lasted until his death 30 years later.

Bitsy once told me that he had wanted to go to Georgia instead of North Carolina because almost all of his Atlanta boyhood friends went to Georgia, not only Malon Courts but also the Boland brothers, Kels and Joe, who were football stars at Georgia as well as tennis lettermen.

But Bitsy went to Carolina because the Tar Heels had the top tennis program in the South, headed by one of the few professional coaches in the country, John Kenfield, who is in the Collegiate Tennis Hall of Fame along with his two most famous protégés, Bitsy Grant and Vic Seixas. Both Bitsy and

Bitsy Grant (second from left) with Dan Magill, Lou Schopfer and Tom Bird — 1967 Southern Men's (45) semifinalists.

Seixas were finalists in the NCAA championships, Bitsy in 1930 and Seixas in both 1947 and 1948.

When I was trying to build up interest in our Crackerland Championships in Athens I implored Bitsy to play in it himself. He and Bobby Dodd won the men's 45 doubles, and Bitsy even played in the men's open singles at age 49, but he lost in the quarters to Lex Hester, then a star at Florida State University.

In 1972, when we first hosted the NCAA championships in Athens, Bitsy again helped us out by being the chair umpire for the singles finals between Trinity teammates Dick Stockton and Brian Gottfried. Being a very shy person, Bitsy really did not like to umpire matches, but he would not turn down requests from friends.

In the late 1960s, when I had begun playing senior tennis, I had the thrill of facing Bitsy myself. In 1966 we met in the finals of the Southern 45 Indoors at Sewanee, Tenn., and I almost won the first set, losing 9-7, and then he cruised in the second set, 6-1. He had run me into the ground, as was his custom against almost anybody he played. But I was stupid enough to think I could beat him if I got in better shape and that I might be ready for him in the Southern 45 Clay Courts at Jackson, Miss., in May. Sure enough, we met again in the finals. We had a long match, but Bitsy won, 6-4, 6-4. He turned the tide with a shot that is seldom used by players today but ought to be. He used the lob approach to the backhand side, sneaking in behind it and invariably winning the point.

I almost forgot to mention that I was 45 years old then, and Bitsy was 56!

I was in Paris watching Mikael Pernfors compete in the French Open when I learned of Bitsy's death in June 1986. Reading Bitsy's long obituary in the paper that morning, I mentioned to Mikael that I wished he could have seen Bitsy play in his prime. They were similar backcourt battlers, and Mikael at five-seven was only three inches taller. Just a year earlier, in May 1985 when Bitsy was inducted into the Collegiate Tennis Hall of Fame during the NCAAs in Athens, I paired Mikael and Bitsy in the Celebrity Doubles, and they formed a mutual admiration society. There is a very good photograph of them together in the Hall of Fame's main display room, as well as the last racquet that Bitsy used, thoughtfully presented to us by Bitsy Grant Tennis Center professional Peter Howell. It was a Kramer Pro Staff, the same model that John McEnroe used in winning the 1978 NCAAs.

And speaking of the Tennis Center, one of Bitsy's lifelong friends, perhaps his closest, was the illustrious Atlanta financier Malon Courts (the Southern Conference champion at Georgia in 1927). Malon became chairman of the Atlanta

Bitsy and Mikael Pernfors playing Celebrity Doubles at the 1985 Hall of Fame ceremonies.

City Parks and Recreation Committee, and he was responsible for getting the magnificent tennis center built on Northside Drive in 1953, which he named for his friend: The Bitsy Grant Tennis Center. It was certainly a fitting tribute to the greatest player ever to come from the state of Georgia, if not the entire South.

Bitsy's great-grandfather, Lemuel P. Grant, was a railroad builder and Civil War figure who donated the land for Atlanta's famous Grant Park. His father, Bryan M. Grant, Sr., was an outstanding player himself. He and Nat Thornton of Atlanta won the Southern Men's doubles four times, and they also were the first Southerners to reach the finals of the U.S. Championships, losing to the four-time champions Fred Alexander and Harold Hackett at Newport in 1907.

Bitsy was only 16 in 1927 when he won his first major title: the Southern Men's singles, which he was to capture a record 11 times during a 25-year span. He was nearing his 42nd birthday when he won for the last time on a hot June Sunday in Memphis in '52; in the semifinals he defeated former Georgia Tech star and future Southern champion Frank Willett, and in the finals he downed ex-Southeastern Conference champion and former Tulane star Leslie Longshore, 6-2, 6-4, 0-6, 6-1.

His best surface was the red clay that abounds in his native Piedmont area of Georgia, and he won the U.S. Men's Clay Court singles three times in his prime (1930, '34 and '35) and the doubles once with the great George Lott in 1932. Bitsy was a first-class doubles player, too. He especially concentrated on doubles when he was past his prime for men's open singles.

Former world champion Bobby Riggs, himself a three-time U.S. Clay Court champion, when asked to name the best clay-court player in history, replied, "I'd say Bitsy Grant and Bjorn Borg. Bitsy was the best I ever played on clay, and Borg won the world's clay-court championship (the French Open) six times. However, I don't think Bitsy ever played in the French Open; he was always busy at the time either playing college matches or playing Davis Cup zone matches."

The clay-court tournament with one of the toughest fields every year is the River Oaks Invitational in Houston, which Bitsy won four times, the last being at age 40 in 1950 over the U.S. men's champion Art Larsen.

J. Donald Budge, the first man to win the Grand Slam, once was asked why he never could win the only major tournament to escape his grasp (the U.S. Clay Court singles), and he replied, "Bitsy Grant."

Bitsy defeated a young Budge in the finals of the 1934 U.S. Clay Courts. And later, when Budge was in his prime, the little Georgian defeated the lanky California redhead in several memorable finals on clay: 1936 at White Sulphur Springs, W.Va., in five furious sets; in straight sets in 1937 at the Miami Biltmore tournament, 6-2, 7-5, 6-0 (one of the few times Budge ever failed to win a set in his long career); and again the next week in the Dixie finals at Tampa, 4-6, 6-3, 6-3, 2-6, 6-2.

In addition to Budge and Riggs, Bitsy had another outstanding rival on clay in the 1930s: Frankie Parker, five-time U.S. Clay Court winner and two-time French champion. They waged some of the longest matches in history: 1937 semifinals of the Dixie at Tampa, Grant winning, 6-3, 6-3, 2-6, 3-6, 6-0, and in the 1939 Tri-State finals at Cincinnati, Bitsy again triumphing, 4-6, 6-3, 6-1, 2-6, 6-4, a match that lasted four hours and 10 minutes (the longest on record at that time).

Bitsy was unbeaten in all six matches on clay in his Davis Cup competition in 1935 and 1936.

As for senior events, he won the U.S. 45 singles on clay six times and the doubles seven times: first with Malon Courts and six times with Larry Shippey.

In the early 1970s Bitsy began developing cataracts, and he won only three more U.S. championships in singles, all on clay: the 60 in 1971, and the 65 in 1976 and 1977.

Like Br'er Rabbit, Bitsy may have been in the "briar patch" playing on clay courts, but he also had many superb performances on grass. In fact, his most notable victory was on grass at Forest Hills, N.Y., on September 7, 1933, against world champion Ellsworth Vines (considered the hardest hitter in tennis annals) in the quarters of the U.S. championships. Vines had won the two previous U.S. singles and also Wimbledon the previous year, but he fell to the indefatigable Bitsy in straight sets, 6-3, 6-3, 6-3.

Grantland Rice, dean of American sportswriters, covered that Vines-Grant match and wrote: "Bitsy Grant, the Georgia jackrabbit, this mighty midget, gave an exhibition of covering the court, of getting the ball back into play, that has never been surpassed, not even by the fast, long-legged Bill Tilden at his best. Little Grant started in a snow-white suit. He finished with a mottled garment covered with mud, grass stains and common dirt. He reminded you of a ball player who had been sliding to second or the plate for a week."

In Rice's memoirs on great champions he had seen in all sports, he wrote: "Pound for pound, at five-four and 120 pounds, Bryan Grant was the fightingest machine I ever saw."

Bobby Dodd, Georgia Tech's longtime football coach, who played doubles with Grant and the other outstanding Atlanta seniors of that era, paid Bitsy this powerful tribute: "Bryan Grant was the finest athlete, any sport and any size, I have seen in my lifetime."

Two of the finest matches Bitsy ever played, both on grass in the U.S. Championships at Forest Hills, he lost in five sets. In 1934 he and Budge had a titanic struggle that Budge recalled in paying tribute to Bitsy following his death:

"We were engaged in a seesaw fight, and late in the fifth set I finally worked up to match point, hitting an overhead smash that I thought was a sure winner. Furthermore, Bitsy had slipped on the wet grass (it had rained all day) and lost his racquet. When I saw him go down, I threw my racquet into the air in a victory gesture. I was sure I had beaten him, but Bitsy frantically crawled on his knees after the ball and somehow got the ball back over the net, and there I was without my racquet. Rain later postponed the match to the next day, and I eked out a hard-earned win."

Budge and Grant were teammates on the victorious Davis

Cup team that finally regained the cup for the U.S. in 1937 after an 11-year hiatus. In one of their toughest matches they upset Australia, which had beaten the U.S. the previous year. It was on grass at Forest Hills and the Aussies were led by the great Jack Crawford (former Wimbledon champion) and the two-handed wizard Jack Bromwich. Bitsy beat Bromwich the first day, 6-2, 7-5, 6-1, and Crawford the final day, 6-0, 6-2, 7-5.

In the next Davis Cup round that summer, against Germany to decide who would challenge champion Great Britain for the Cup, Bitsy suffered one of the most disappointing losses of his career to the great German champion, Baron von Cramm, losing in straight sets. Von Cramm was favored to win, but Bitsy himself was confident he could topple the German. Several months later, though, in the semifinals of the U.S. Championships at Forest Hills — again on grass — Bitsy fought his heart out trying to avenge that loss to von Cramm and he almost did! But von Cramm won in five sets, 9-7, 2-6, 2-6, 6-3, 6-3.

The *New York Times'* famed tennis writer, Allison Danzig, termed it one of the greatest matches ever played at Forest Hills, and Bitsy himself said, "It was the best tennis I ever played."

If so, how I wish I had it on film.

BIG BILL TILDEN

When I was a boy, playing in the state high school tournament on Georgia's old red clay courts in the late 1930s, none other than Big Bill Tilden and his professional troupe of players showed up and were seated on benches right by the court on which I was playing. They were in town for an exhibition match to be played that night on the floor of our basketball court.

A few minutes later I noticed Tilden smiling and talking to his main sparring partner Vinnie Richards. I thought they were talking about me and laughing at the way I hit the ball. Subsequent events proved that assumption to be correct. After my match, when I happened to walk by Tilden and his troupe, Big Bill himself beckoned for me to come over. He said to me, "Young man, we were quite amused by the unique method you use to hit a tennis ball. I have never seen a person choke the racquet as high up as you do."

Actually, I did choke the racquet quite a bit. I gripped it almost at the racquet's throat — the same as I did a ping-pong paddle. I had played ping-pong all my life at the Athens YMCA but knew next to nothing about how to grip a tennis racquet or stroke a tennis ball. There weren't any professional tennis teachers in Athens in those days.

Tilden went on to say, "If you would grip the racquet at the end of the handle, you'd have a lot more reach and also more leverage, so you could get more pace on the ball."

I thanked him for the advice, and then he asked me if I would round up some ball boys for their match that night. I was happy to do so, and after the match he gave all the ball boys some of the match balls and gave me one of his old Spalding racquets. Later I tried to grip the racquet as Tilden suggested, but I liked my way better.

Three years later, when I was a Georgia freshman, our freshman coach, Dr. Robert H. West, told me the same thing Tilden had, and I said to Dr. West, "Ty Cobb choked his bat in baseball." To which Dr. West replied, "Baseball is not the same as tennis, and, furthermore, YOU'RE NO TY COBB."

But back to Bill Tilden. He actually brought his touring professionals to the University of Georgia campus twice: 1936 and 1938. He played Vincent Richards one time and Bruce Barnes the next, but I knew so little about tennis that I couldn't appreciate his shots. I do recall his knocking the heck out of his serve for a lot of aces, but what I remember best was a trick shot he executed. Undoubtedly he had prearranged this act. For in the middle of a game, Tilden stopped play and yelled to a boy hawking peanuts to "pipe down." But the boy kept on walking alongside the court, yelling at the top of his voice, "PEANUTS HERE. TEN CENTS A PACK." All of a sudden Big Bill hauled off and drove a ball straight at the boy and knocked the sack of peanuts right out of his hand. The crowd let go with a tremendous cheer, and Big Bill strutted back to the match.

I only saw Tilden play one other time: December 1945 at the famed Los Angeles Tennis Club in the World's Professional Hardcourt championships. In addition to Tilden, who was 51 years old and had just been voted the greatest player in the history of the game, the field included former world champion Fred Perry, current champion Don Budge, who had just returned home from World War II, and the up-and-coming, soon-to-be-world-champion Bobby Riggs, also fresh home from Navy duty.

I was in San Diego, just back in the states after Marine service in the Pacific, and I read about the tournament in a San Diego newspaper. I talked a fellow officer, Lt. George Costopolous of Boston, into making the short bus trip to Los Angeles, where we saw the quarters, the semis and the finals. Tilden upset a younger Lester Stoefen in the quarters, then lost to Budge in the semis while Riggs was beating Perry. Riggs then toppled Budge in the finals. But I was amazed to see Tilden keep the great Budge on the defensive throughout most of their match, losing crucial points by only an inch or so. Later Tilden came back to beat a much younger Perry in the third-place playoff.

One thing I remember about Tilden was the fact that he seemed to glide around the court so effortlessly. He had tremendous speed, agility, and grace. I had always heard that he was the best athlete in the game and that the track coach at the University of Pennsylvania, where Bill had played tennis for a year, had told Bill that he could make a national quarter-mile champion out of him if he'd quit tennis and concentrate on track.

In Bobby Riggs' fine book, *Tennis Is My Racket*, I was

"Big Bill" Tilden (r) with "Little Bill" Johnston at the U.S. Open finals.

pleased that Riggs called Tilden the greatest player of all time. "From the matches I have played against him and seen him play against others," wrote Riggs, "I am convinced that if Bill could be so good in his early 50s, he must have been nothing short of colossal when he was in his 20s. You can talk about

Cochet, Vines, Johnston, Perry, Budge, Kramer — they all were great. But in my book Tilden stands far above them all."

"KING" DAVID BENJAMIN

In 1957, J. D. Morgan, UCLA's great tennis coach and athletic director, originated the National Intercollegiate Tennis Coaches Association, now known as ITCA. Appropriately, ITCA's highest award today is named for J. D. Morgan.

In 1991 I had the great privilege of helping bestow this high honor on a coach cut from the same fabric as the accomplished Morgan. In fact, this coach's contributions to collegiate tennis, in my opinion, are unequalled. I speak of the executive director of the Intercollegiate Tennis Coaches' Association, and head tennis coach at Princeton University, the indefatigable and incomparable David A. Benjamin.

When I think of David Benjamin, I think of him first as a star player for Harvard, whose teams Coach Jack Barnaby brought to Athens early each spring back in the 1960s. I vividly remember the baseline battles David played against Georgia's No. 1 player, the late Henry Feild. We had clay courts then, and David and Henry played two of the longest matches in the history of our stadium. We badly needed no-ad scoring when those two mighty battlers fought it out. They could run down everything — and forever.

When David became Princeton's coach in 1974, I had the pleasure of seeing him again at the Princeton Indoors each February. Immediately he did a superb job with both the Tigers' squash and tennis programs, and a few years later — when I was chairman of the NCAA Tennis Committee — I needed to appoint a member from the East. Without hesitation, I asked the brightest young coach in the country to serve, and he accepted. Today I proudly claim David

Benjamin as my protégé. His peers soon realized his many talents, and they voted him president of the coaches' association and re-elected him. Eventually they asked him to be our first executive director. He has been the best thing that has ever happened to our national program. I believe that is the unanimous opinion of all coaches who have known him.

Jack Barnaby coached Harvard tennis for some 40 years, and he told me once that David was the smartest boy and most respected by his teammates of any player he had ever coached.

It stands to reason that David graduated *magna cum laude* at Harvard in American history and literature, was a finalist in the Rhodes Scholarship competition and received a fellowship for study at Trinity College in Cambridge, England.

Perhaps the three best players David has had at Princeton

David Benjamin (l) with Ted Farnsworth, Mikael Pernfors and Dan Magill at the Princeton Indoors.

were All-Americans Leif Shiras (today a noted TV commentator on tennis), Jay Lapidus, and Ted Farnsworth; and each of them has told me that David had an uncanny ability to instill confidence in his players. Lapidus, now coach at Duke University, said that when David sat on the court for his matches he felt he couldn't lose.

On the way out to Austin for that ceremony back in 1991, it dawned upon me why David Benjamin is a great leader and why he is so wise in making the many daily decisions required of him as ITCA's chief executive officer. It's because of the pressure put on him when his father, Rabbi Benjamin, named him for the little shepherd boy who slung the stone that slew the Philistine giant Goliath and went on to become the greatest king in the history of his people. And, of course, King David's son was Solomon, the very wisest of kings.

There's another reason David Benjamin is so brilliant. He is bound to be a direct descendent of the Confederate States of America's great statesman, Judah Benjamin, the distinguished South Carolinian who was secretary of war, secretary of state, and attorney general in Jefferson Davis's cabinet.

It was only appropriate, then, that college tennis's highest honor should go to Coach David Benjamin, King of College Tennis.

HENRY FEILD,
"THE LITTLE PROFESSOR"

The University of Georgia's tennis stadium, the site of 17 NCAA men's tennis championships, was named for an Athens native who learned to play on the Bulldogs' courts and later starred three years as their No. 1 player: the late Henry Spottswood Feild, who died in an automobile accident in Atlanta on January 1, 1968.

His father, David Meade Feild, was a distinguished law professor at Georgia. A native Virginian who did his undergraduate studies at North Carolina and his law work at Harvard, Prof. Feild was a descendent of one of Virginia's most illustrious colonial governors, Henry Spottswood, for whom he named his youngest son.

Prof. Feild, a devoted tennis fan who never missed one of his son's matches, loved to tease both Henry and me whenever Georgia played Harvard, and Henry hooked up with The Crimson's No. 1 player, David Benjamin, back in 1965 and 1966.

"I'll be forced to pull for Harvard today, Dan. That's my alma mater, you know," he would say with a twinkle in his eye.

Henry stood only five-four and weighed only 120 pounds, but he was a very good, quick, smart athlete. In college he took up weightlifting in a P.E. class and he became quite muscular and strong for his size. He also took a P.E. wrestling class and was so good that varsity coach Sam Mrvos thought he could become conference champion as his 118-pounder.

I told Sam, "Hell, no. He's already our No. 1 tennis player; he hasn't got any time for wrestling."

Henry was one of several Athens boys who were just taking up tennis when I began coaching Georgia's varsity in 1955. The others included Freddie Birchmore, Jr., whose brother Danny would later make All-America at Georgia; Charley Hooper, Jr., whose father had captained Georgia's tennis team in the 1920s; Alex Keller, whose father Dr. Paul Keller was my lifelong friend and later my senior doubles partner; Albert Jones, Jr., son of former Georgia tennis captain and coach and one of my closest friends for many years; and my own son Ham, a year younger than the other boys.

I think I had more fun coaching those boys than anything else I have done in tennis. They were all bright boys and outstanding students, and they were the best group I ever had in learning "percentage tennis." I used to punish them whenever they made a stupid shot in practice — like driving through an opponent in commanding position at net instead of lobbing — by having them run laps or do push-ups or pick up cigarette butts in the clubhouse area.

I also would give them the same punishment if they cursed or threw their racquets or engaged in any other kind of poor sportsmanship. I guess I thought I was still in the Marine Corps because I relished making men out of them. Two of my protégés won the coveted Tom Stowe Sportsmanship Award at the national juniors in Kalamazoo: Billy Lenoir in 1960 and Danny Birchmore in 1969. But I must confess they were well-disciplined, fine boys when I began working with them (thanks to their parents).

Henry's first tournament match was the Crackerland Boys' 13 singles in 1957, where he lost to Hugh Hailey of Atlanta in the first round. Five years later he beat Hugh (later to play for me at UGA on the same team with Henry) in the finals of the Georgia high school tournament, 7-5, 5-7, 6-4.

The best player in the Southeastern Conference during Henry's collegiate career was Walter Johnson of Georgia Tech. When Henry was a freshman (frosh were not eligible for the varsity in those days), he had a dual match record of 12-2. Both losses were to Johnson, who also nipped Henry in the finals of the SEC Freshman No. 1 singles.

Henry played the No. 1 position on the UGA varsity three straight years, leading the Bulldogs to their most successful consecutive seasons ever at that time: 17-3 in 1964, splitting two engagements with arch rival Johnson; 19-2 in 1965, losing twice to Johnson, one by 15-13, 7-5; and 19-3 in 1966, losing a heartbreaker to Johnson in Atlanta, 6-3, 4-6, 9-7. Henry held a 4-1 lead in the final set when he was struck by severe cramps in both legs and racquet hand.

Henry played some of his best tennis during the summer of

1966, following his graduation at Georgia. He reached the finals of the Georgia State Open in Macon and also the finals of the Crackerland, defeating future SEC champion Tommy Mozur of Tennessee in the semis, then losing in the finals to North Carolina's ace, Gene Hamilton.

In the summer of 1967 Henry played only two tournaments, reaching the finals of both the State Closed in Macon and the State Open in Atlanta, where he lost to John Skogstad in the finals after having upset former SEC champion Ned Neely of Georgia Tech, 2-6, 6-4, 7-5.

Henry's charming wit and impeccable sportsmanship endeared him to teammates, opponents and fans. One of his biggest admirers was Georgia Tech coach Jack Rodgers, who

Magill (c) with home-grown products (l-r) Henry Feild, Alex Keller, Freddie Birchmore and Albert Jones, 1962 Southern Prep champs.

nicknamed him "the Little Professor."

The late *Atlanta Journal* sportswriter Guy Tiller referred to Henry as the "Court Jester" of the Bulldogs. It really was a joy to be with him on tennis trips. He was a gifted mimic, simply hilarious in imitating Little Richard, Louis Armstrong, and Presidents Kennedy and Johnson.

He also was a talented artist. During the Christmas holidays of 1967, just a few days before his fatal accident on New Year's Day, he had almost completed a fine portrait of his father.

Henry had too much fun in college and was too busy with his tennis to make the outstanding grades his older sister Madge did (she was a top honor graduate in the Georgia Law School), but Henry told me that he was going to make up for lost time at Mercer University's law school, where he was enrolled at the time of his death. He definitely planned to follow in his father's footsteps.

Georgia Athletic Director Joel Eaves was a great admirer of Henry and seldom missed watching him play. A few days after Henry's death Coach Eaves called me into his office and said, "Dan, what do you think about our naming the tennis stadium for Henry?"

I do believe naming our stadium for Henry was the best thing Coach Eaves and I ever did.

DANNY BIRCHMORE,
GEORGIA'S FIRST ALL-AMERICAN

In the late 1950s I began coaching an Athens boy who had some of the qualities indicative of a national champion. His father, Fred Birchmore, Sr., must have thought the youngest of his four children was destined for greatness. He named him Daniel Alexander Birchmore for the biblical hero Daniel and for the immortal warrior Alexander the Great.

Little Danny was only six when he took up tennis. Unlike Billy Lenoir, my first national junior champion, Danny used only one hand — the conventional method — to hit the ball. Although he never could stroke the ball with the fluidness or pace that Lenoir could, he was faster in covering the court and he was just as steady as Billy. Both also had the heart of a lion, an absolutely necessary ingredient for a champion.

Danny was not a natural shotmaker. He developed an unusual style of blocking the ball on his ground strokes instead of really stroking the ball in the classical manner. But he did block through the ball and he had uncanny timing on hitting the ball on the rise most of the time, which gave his shots good pace. His backhand was very strong, and his footwork was as good as I have ever seen.

While compiling a brilliant record in Georgia junior play, Danny also managed to skip a grade along the way, so he was only 17 when he entered Georgia in the fall of 1968. Georgia switched from clay to hard courts this very year, and, since he had always been a clay-court baseliner, I was afraid Danny would not have the power or net game to be a good hard-court player. But it soon became evident that Danny's "block strokes" were made to order for volleying, and he immediately became an expert volleyer.

Danny played No. 1 as a Georgia freshman during the spring of 1969, wresting the top spot from the No. 1 Bulldog of the two previous years, the talented Bill Shippey. He had a good year in dual matches, posting a 14-4 mark, and he gave ultimate champion Armi Neely of Florida a tough match in the SEC semifinals, bowing 6-4, 8-6. He also made a fine showing in the NCAAs at Princeton, losing to defending champion Bob Lutz of USC in the fourth round.

I believe it was the tough competition Danny had at No. 1 singles his freshman year that enabled him to win the National Boys' 18 Clay Court singles that summer in Louisville. He was the only boy in the tournament who had played college tennis, and he dominated the field without dropping a set. In the quarters he upset none other than Jimmy Connors of St. Louis, and then beat Harold Solomon of Silver Springs, Md., in the finals, 6-3, 8-6.

Danny had a super junior year in 1971, leading Georgia to its first-ever SEC team title, winning the No. 1 singles and

No. 1 doubles (with Norm Holmes). At the NCAAs he advanced to the round of 16, where he just barely lost to Trinity star Paul Gerken, 1-6, 7-5, 6-2. In fact, Danny actually played an out ball on his own match point in the second set; having linesmen on duty would have brought him a great victory.

But Danny came back with Norm Holmes to upset USC's Marcello Lara and Dick Bohrnstedt to reach the quarters of the doubles, and they became Georgia's first All-Americans in tennis. Danny also was voted by the players and coaches the most coveted honor in collegiate tennis: the Rafael Osuna Award for sportsmanship and competitive excellence.

That summer he won the U.S. Junior Davis Cup singles and doubles (with Raz Reid) at Poughkeepsie, N.Y. Then, in the National Amateur Clay Court Championships, he scored one of his greatest victories ever, upsetting the No. 1 seed and defending champion Roscoe Tanner, 7-6, 6-4, — in Roscoe's hometown of Chattanooga, too.

During Danny's four years at Georgia, 1968 through 1972, he was the main "drawing card" as Georgia set national collegiate attendance records for its home matches. Often there were crowds of over 2,000 (mostly students) watching from the grassy hillside overlooking the courts. Also during Danny's era Georgia set a school record (in all sports) by winning 76 consecutive dual matches at home. The streak was snapped April 27, 1972, when a crowd of 3,000-plus came out to see Miami's perennial powerhouse, led by future U.S. top-tenner Eddie Dibbs, win a hard-fought match, 6-3. The feature match between Danny and Eddie was a thriller, barely won by the great Dibbs, 7-5, 4-6, 6-4.

A month later Danny hoped very much to make a strong showing for the home fans in the NCAAs, which were held on Georgia's courts for the first time. In one of the strongest fields in NCAA history, Danny won four matches to reach

Danny Birchmore wins the Rafael Osuna Award in 1971.

the round of 16, where he lost a close battle, 6-3, 6-4, to his longtime foe, Stanford's mighty Roscoe Tanner. If the surface had been clay, Danny might have been able to duplicate his great victory of the previous summer over Roscoe.

Danny's tremendous academic achievement won him an NCAA post-graduate scholarship, so he passed up his chance for a career in professional tennis. He studied medicine and ·

now is practicing rheumatology at a Veterans' Hospital in Delaware. I surely do wish he'd return to his hometown and look after his old and aching coach.

MIKAEL PERNFORS, TWO-TIME NCAA CHAMPION

The very first time I saw Mikael Pernfors hit a tennis ball I knew Georgia had a genuine "blue chipper." In early September 1983 the diminutive Swede arrived in Athens for our annual boot camp, consisting of two-a-day drills a week prior to the opening of school. I recall saying to our assistant coach and former All-American Manuel Diaz, "We're lucky. This boy is as agile and as quick a player as I have ever seen, and his forehand drives — both flat and top spin — are tremendous."

We were lucky because I had awarded Pernfors a scholarship "sight unseen," having taken the word of two friends that he'd be good enough to make our team; but I had been unable to see him play when he visited our camps in December 1982, it being against NCAA rules for a prospect to "work out."

I expected him to be a tough player, though, because he had never lost a junior college match in two years. But I was not expecting him to supplant Allen Miller, NCAA doubles champion and also an All-American in singles in 1983, as our No. 1 player. However, after watching Pernfors show me his repertoire of shots during that first workout in Athens, I said to Coach Diaz, "This boy has the ability to be our No. 1 player." And after his second practice, I declared to one of our most loyal supporters, retired English Department head Dr. Robert West: "Pernfors is good enough to win the NCAAs," and added, jokingly, "He's caught on to my coaching faster than anybody I've ever had."

Pernfors originally was recommended to me by his coach, Larry Castle of Seminole Junior College in Samford, Fla., whom I had known when he starred in basketball and baseball at Western Kentucky and later when he coached tennis at East Tennessee State and Middle Tennessee State before moving to Florida. I had another strong recommendation from Paul Groth, co-captain of Georgia's 1981 SEC championship team who had lost to Pernfors in the finals of an open tournament at Harbor Beach, Fla., in the fall of 1982. Paul pointed out that Pernfors had beaten a highly regarded Australian pro, David Carter, in this tournament and that, in his opinion, Pernfors would be the best player Georgia ever had.

So I decided to offer Pernfors a scholarship when he visited us in December 1982. He accepted, and I'm sure he enjoyed his stay in Athens. His student host was the genial giant Ola Malmqvist, a fellow Swede who also had played junior college tennis in Florida. However, they had not known each other until meeting in Athens. Both were to become NCAA champions.

Pernfors made a brilliant debut at Georgia, winning three of four tournaments in the fall of '83. He captured the Clemson Classic against a tough field that included another Swede, Fredrik Pahlett of Minnesota (finalist in the 1983 NCAA singles), Lawson Duncan of Clemson who was finalist to Pernfors eight months later in the 1984 NCAAs, and his own talented teammate Allen Miller, whom he defeated in the finals.

The next week in Athens Pernfors won an even bigger tournament: the Southern Collegiates, beating Mike Smith of Duke in the finals; he also won the doubles with Miller. He played three more events that fall and established himself as one of the very top collegians in the country. At Los Angeles in the Nike All-American he reached the quarters before losing a heartbreaker to Todd Witsken of Southern Cal, 6-7, 6-4, 6-4 (cramps handicapped him in the final set). In mid-November he won the ITCA Region Three Indoors on his home courts, defeating All-American Andy Solis of Alabama in the semis and teammate Miller in the final. He and Miller won the doubles.

In February '84 Pernfors won the tough Princeton Indoors, his victim in the finals being the defending champion Ted Farnsworth of Princeton, the 1983 ITCA National Indoor champion, 6-2, 2-6, 6-3.

In Georgia's first outdoor dual match of the spring Pernfors lost another heartbreaker to the nation's No. 1 ranked player, Paul Annacone of Tennessee (later to reach the quarterfinals at Wimbledon), 5-7, 7-6, 7-6. Pernfors had two match points in the final set at 5-6, but cramps in his right hand kept him from scoring a great victory.

Pernfors was particularly outstanding in late March at Montgomery where he was unbeaten and voted the MVP in the Blue-Gray Team Tournament. He got revenge on Auburn's Dan Cassady, who had beaten him in the semifinals of the SEC Indoors in January. But the grueling four-day tournament was costly. He was too worn out to play his best two days later against Clemson's powerful Lawson Duncan, and he got crushed 6-2, 6-1 before his home fans. He wouldn't give an alibi, but he was hoping to get another crack at Duncan in the NCAAs.

Pernfors led Georgia to the 1984 SEC round-robin dual match crown that spring and also the NCAA Region Three team title. In the SEC Outdoor individual championships at Tuscaloosa he lost another tough three-setter to top-ranked Annacone, 1-6, 6-2, 6-3.

Then followed the biggest tournament of all: the 100th NCAAs in his own backyard at Henry Feild Stadium, where he simply played the greatest tennis of his life. He won 10 straight singles matches against the best amateurs in the world: four in the team tournament and six more in the singles tournament.

In the team tournament he defeated Kelly Evernden of Arkansas, Matt Anger of USC, Dan Goldie of Stanford, and Jerome Jones of Pepperdine. He then streamrolled through the individual tournament, defeating Mark Styslinger of SMU; Jon Treml of NE Louisiana; Jeff Klaparda of UCLA; Todd Witsken of USC, avenging the loss in the Nike at Los Angeles in the fall; John Levine of Texas in a cliff-hanger, 1-6, 7-6, 6-2; and Lawson Duncan of Clemson in the finals, 6-1, 6-4.

The finals were witnessed by an overflow crowd of 4,500, the largest ever to see a collegiate tennis match at that time (but eclipsed the next year when Georgia beat UCLA in the team tournament finals). Duncan had reached the final round by winning over Auburn's outstanding South African Barry Moir, who had toppled the top seed Annacone in the quarters.

We "cooked up" some special strategy for Pernfors to use against Duncan, whose game was built around a mighty forehand that he loved to hit inside-out from the backhand corner after stepping around his much weaker backhand side. I knew exactly how to play this type of forehand slugger, having been jerked around the court myself many times by the outstanding Atlanta senior Tom Bird, possessor of one of the hardest forehand drives in Southern tennis history. The best way to counteract a player who steps around his backhand and controls play with his big forehand is to hit the ball as soon as possible to your opponent's forehand corner, forcing him to hit his next shot on the run. This maneuver gets your opponent out of his pet backhand corner position and enables you to finally attack his weaker backhand side.

In a special pre-match practice Assistant Coach Diaz and I had discussed this battle plan with Pernfors, and also with my longtime friend Jack Waters, the distinguished veteran pro at

Mikael Pernfors giving his famous "Swedish salute" to the crowd.

the Atlanta Piedmont Driving Club, who was on hand for the match. Jack through the years had sent me a number of his protégés, seven of whom later captained Georgia teams.

Of course, plans are easy to make but not as easy to execute. However, Pernfors executed well enough to win numerous points and — equally important — he managed to run Duncan out of his pet position on the court. He did it with backhand slices down the line and powerful forehand drives crosscourt.

We also had noticed that Duncan's position in receiving serve, in either court, left his forehand side vulnerable to a good slice serve to the alley in the deuce court and a well-paced serve down the centerstripe in the "ad" court. So Pernfors attacked these spots with his serve and profited a number of times, including the last point of the match: an ace in the deuce court.

Pernfors no doubt benefited somewhat from Duncan's overconfidence. The Clemson star had rolled to an easy victory over the little Swede on the same courts six weeks earlier. But on that occasion Pernfors was tired from four days' hard play in the Blue-Gray tournament and also had a touch of the flu. This time, though, Duncan faced the real Mikael Pernfors at the top of his game — highly psyched by that great motivator: *sweet revenge.*

Once Mikael captured the coveted singles crown in 1984, he was pounced upon by sports agents, all trying to sign him to a professional contract and get him to relinquish his final year of eligibility at the University of Georgia. Of course, all of us at Georgia hoped he would return for his senior season, but we would not have begrudged his leaving us. After all, Jimmy Connors of UCLA turned pro after winning the NCAAs as a freshman in 1971, as did John McEnroe of Stanford in 1978, and they are still revered at their respective alma maters.

We knew, of course, that if Pernfors returned to defend his title, the odds would be overwhelmingly against his repeating. Winning back-to-back NCAA singles titles is a feat that has been accomplished by only two players since World War II. Tulane's Ham Richardson did it in 1953 and 1954, and USC's Dennis Ralston in 1963 and 1964.

I simply told Mikael that, if he turned pro, all his Georgia friends would wish him the best of luck, and I also told him that I thought another season of college tennis would better prepare him for a professional career. I sincerely believed he needed to be a more disciplined player in his choice of shots, a better percentage player.

Several days later (it was June 1984), Mikael and his roommate, fellow Swede Ola Malmqvist, dropped by my home for a visit, at which time Mikael told me that he had made his decision.

"I want to stay at Georgia," he said matter-of-factly, following which I embraced him not so matter-of-factly. I was jubilant!

When he returned to Athens in September 1984 for our annual pre-season "boot camp," Mikael had a new roommate. Senior George Bezecny of Fort Lauderdale, Fla., replaced the big Swede Ola Malmqvist, who had graduated and begun a coaching career.

Bezecny's rooming with Pernfors turned out to be one of the best "coaching" moves I ever made. Bezecny was a fine boy of high character, but he was extremely shy and had roomed by himself off campus three straight years. I believed that he brooded when he lost matches and was lonely living by himself. I thought that rooming with the high-spirited and playful Pernfors would be enjoyable and good in many ways for Bezecny, and as a result, I also thought, would make Bezecny a better tennis player. Mikael agreed that it was a good idea, and he immediately asked George to room with him.

Although George had been USTA Boys' 16 clay-court singles champion, he had not reached his potential at Georgia. He was No. 4 as a freshman in 1982, No 5. as a sophomore (missing the last half of the season because of a knee operation), and No. 4 again as a junior. Guess what he did his senior year after rooming with Pernfors? That fall he was runner-up to Pernfors in two big tournaments: the Southern Collegiates and the Rider-Rolex at LaFayette, La. What's more, he won the tough Region Three Indoors (Pernfors didn't play), and that spring he played No. 2 on Georgia's best team ever.

But back to Pernfors. In the fall of '84 he began his fabulous collegiate "swan song" by winning three big tournaments: the Southern Collegiate, in which he nipped roommate Bezecny in the finals; the fast Rider-Rolex in LaFayette, La., where he beat SMU's outstanding Richey Reneberg in

Pernfors gets congratulations on his '84 NCAA title from tennis analysts Cliff Drysdale (r) and Steve Flink.

the semis and then again beat his roommate in the finals; and finally the Volvo All-America (one of the ITCA's Grand Slam events), where he defeated USC's Todd Witsken in a tough three-set final. Back home in Georgia, Mikael won two more matches in the Georgia Tech team tournament to run his fall record to an astonishing 22-0.

After the Christmas break, Pernfors picked up right where he left off, winning the SEC Indoor in Nashville and then taking the ITCA Indoor team tournament in Louisville. But his phenomenal streak finally ended the next week in Houston at the ITCA-Rolex National Indoors. After beating Stanford's big Jim Grabb in a tough three-set semifinal bout, Pernfors succumbed to another Cardinal, Dan Goldie, in the finals. The loss ended his consecutive victory streak at 42. It had begun with a 10-0 mark in the 1984 NCAAs and continued 32 matches into the 1984–85 season.

The spring dual match season now was at hand, and Pernfors won 16 straight before bowing to Chris Kennedy of Trinity in three sets in the Blue-Gray team tournament at Montgomery. Two weeks later he lost for the third and final time of the season. Florida's Shawn Taylor prevailed in Gainesville when I should not have played Mikael, whose old back injury had recurred. But he never lost again, winning his last 18 matches in succession, including the SEC Outdoor finals over Shelby Cannon of Tennessee, 6-4, 6-3, at Baton Rouge, and the NCAA finals over teammate and roommate George Bezecny.

The final tally for the super Swede's sensational senior season: six trophies out of a total of seven tournaments entered. Furthermore, his record for the year was 71-3, a modern collegiate record for a No. 1 player. And by the way, the 42 consecutive wins also set an ICTA national record for a No. 1 player.

Also, the ultimate dream for which he remained at Georgia for his senior year became a reality.

A Few Favorite Stories

MANUEL DIAZ
AND THE MONSTER SERVE

I'll never forget Manuel Diaz' first trip to the University of Georgia, which was in early April 1971 when we were playing a home match against Virginia. I was standing in the lobby of the Henry Feild clubhouse, preparing to introduce the starting lineups, when a tall, handsome boy and his look-alike father came up and introduced themselves. They were Manuel Diaz, Sr., and Manolito, who had just arrived in Athens without advance notice. They wanted to see where Manolito was considering spending his next four years. (I had offered Manolito a scholarship, sight unseen, based on the great recommendation of one of my former players, Tony Ortiz.)

I was happy to see them, and they must have enjoyed the visit because Manolito, when he returned to San Juan a few days later, mailed me back his signed Southeastern Conference grant-in-aid.

Manuel came to Athens with the rudiments of a great

topspin serve, taught him by Welby Van Horn; and he was a fine, strong, and fleet athlete who was a natural net rusher and volleyer and who could jump unusually high to put away overheads. He had a beautiful sliced backhand approach, but was a little crude on his forehand drive and forehand service return.

His main weakness as a freshman was nervousness. He tried too hard and was so uptight that he had frequent nose-bleeding, and we always had to have a roll of toilet paper at courtside.

Manuel jumped from No. 6 to our No. 1 spot his sophomore year (after the graduation of All-American Danny Birchmore), and he won his first big tournament in February 1973, the Princeton Indoors. In May at Vanderbilt he led Georgia to its third straight SEC team title, capturing the No. 1 singles and No. 2 doubles with Bill Kopecky.

He began his junior season in October 1973 by beating Kopecky in three sets in the Southern Collegiate finals, and he also repeated as Princeton Indoor champion, again nipping teammate Kopecky in a three-set final; but Big Bill edged Manuel two close challenge matches to one to get the No. 1 singles spot on the team. Manuel went on to win the SEC No. 2 singles and No. 1 doubles with Kopecky as Georgia won its fourth straight SEC team crown.

As a senior Manuel had one of the finest seasons ever by a Bulldog player. He began by repeating as Southern Collegiate champion, edging North Carolina State's powerful John Sadri in the finals, and in March 1975 he scored the best victory of his career, upsetting NCAA champion John Whitlinger of Stanford, 7-6, 6-2, before a monstrous crowd of over 3,000 who sat on the hillside overlooking the Georgia courts (the stadium was not built there until two years later). Manuel scorched a devastating 14 aces against Whitlinger and hit the serve so hard that he could barely move his right arm the next day. His arm was so sore that I should have held him out of

Current Bulldog coach Manuel Diaz had a lot to celebrate in '75.

our next two matches — Miami and Florida State — but he wanted to help us win. As a result, he suffered the only two losses of his dual match season.

Later in the season, with his arm healthy again, Manuel

pulled off the most unbelievable serve I have ever seen. It came against a powerful Pepperdine team coached by Larry Riggs, son of the famous world champion Bobby Riggs, and a big crowd was on hand to see the duel at No. 1 singles between two of the country's greatest collegians, both Latin Americans: Georgia's Manuel Diaz and Pepperdine's Joavo Soares, later to star on Brazil's Davis Cup team. Manuel, serving at his very best, won a thrilling match, 7-6, 7-6, the second set tie-breaker going the limit.

Manuel was down, 2-4, but serving in the nine-point tie-breaker. When he knotted the score at 4-points apiece, Soares chose to receive the sudden-death point in the deuce court. Manuel responded by hitting the mightiest topspin serve imaginable. It went crosscourt to Soares' forehand side, bouncing over his head, totally out of his reach, and over a low fence in the corner — plumb out of the arena — and the partisan crowd went nuts. The issue was not quite decided, though, because Manuel's racquet had slipped out of his hand as he struck the ball and it bounced into the net.

Coach Riggs ran up to me and said the point belonged to Soares because Manuel's racquet had hit the net; I told Coach Riggs that I was not the umpire and pointed to Dr. Bill Blackstone in the chair. When Riggs confronted Dr. Blackstone with his protest, Dr. Blackstone (a former Elon College football star of Cherokee blood who looked like an Indian chief) calmly replied: "That's true; his racquet did hit the net but not until the ball had bounced over the fence out of play, ending the point."

Riggs then turned to me, shook my hand and said, "Well, all I've got to say is that it was the damnedest serve I've ever seen."

At the SEC tournament in Tuscaloosa, and again at the NCAAs in Corpus Christi, Manuel was devastated by utter heat prostration. At the SEC he came out of the University of Alabama hospital in time to team with Gordon Smith for the win at No. 1 doubles that clinched Georgia's fifth straight team championship. At the NCAAs he and Smith managed to win four matches, but their last two wins were so grueling that Manuel had to be hospitalized again, and he and Smith were forced to default the quarterfinals without taking the court.

When I picked up Manuel from the hospital in Texas, the doctor shocked me to the core by telling me, "Coach, you almost lost your boy. He had a very close call. He suffered one of the worst cases of heat prostration I have ever seen."

Back in Athens, Manuel took a thorough physical examination, and we learned that his system did not properly replenish lost fluids in extremely hot weather. So, you coaches and players who may be reading this book, remember that hot weather can pose a dangerous health threat.

TERRIBLE TIM DELANEY

If you think John McEnroe had a bad temper, you would be correct. And if you wanted to win a bet about a college player at the same time who had a more volatile temper than the Mighty Mac, you would put your money on Tim Delaney, whose tantrums were so bad his first year at Georgia that I nicknamed him "Mount Vesuvius." However, Tim gradually learned to direct this excessive spirit into the right channels, and following his graduation we named an annual award for him: the Tim Delaney Best Competitor Award.

Although Tim was able to subdue his temper, he was plagued with so many unfortunate injuries that he never won All-America honors — as did his brothers Jim (twice an

NCAA doubles champion at Stanford) and Chris at Southern Methodist. But Tim was a very valuable player in helping Georgia win the SEC team title three of his four years: 1975, '77 and '78.

In 1973, the year before he entered Georgia, Tim won three National Interscholastics doubles titles with younger brother Chris and also reached the singles finals himself. So it was no surprise to me when Tim debuted in the fall Southern Collegiates with a first-round upset of No. 2 seed John Eagleton of Miami.

Talented as Tim was, though, he had to play down at No. 5 as a freshman (behind SEC championship team veterans Manuel Diaz, Gordon Smith, David Dick and Joe Gettys). But he did compile a fine 16-1 record and went undefeated in the SEC round-robin schedule, earning himself the top seed in the SEC tournament at Tuscaloosa in the No. 5 division.

But here, unfortunately, his reputation as a hothead proved his undoing. He was upset in his first match by Kentucky's Steve Gilliam, 4-6, 6-4, 7-5, a player he had beaten earlier that spring in straight sets.

In this infamous "Mt. Vesuvius" match I had stayed with Tim off and on most of the first set, which he won, and I thought he had the match well in hand. So I moved around to watch my other men (this was before coaches had assistants to share in this work). I didn't get back to his match until the final game, but I did see what happened when he left the court. He went straight up to four players of a rival team sitting on the first row of the grandstand by his court, and he began knocking the daylights out of them. In fact, I believe he would have kayoed all of them had not several coaches, myself included, pulled him off.

One of the coaches told me that he didn't blame Delaney at all because these players had heckled him throughout the match (that is, whenever I was not around) and had succeeded in getting him so riled up that he didn't play his best game —

Tim Delaney

and there was no umpire in the chair to stop the hecklers. Nevertheless, Tim's outburst resulted in the Tournament Committee's meeting with SEC Commissioner Boyd McWorter, and they would have disqualified Tim from the doubles event had I not been able to persuade a fellow coach to give "just cause" for Tim's "assault and battery."

Tim was terribly hampered by knee problems his sophomore and junior seasons, though at the end of his junior year he was in good enough form to help us win the SEC title at Gainesville, capturing the No. 6 singles and No. 3 doubles with Elango Ranganathan. As a senior he played No. 2 singles, but his knee bothered him so much he could only be effective at No. 1 doubles with Wesley Cash. They won the Princeton Indoors and reached the finals of the SEC, losing a close three-setter to Tennessee's Tracy DeLatte and John Gillespie.

Another favorite "Mount Vesuvius" story took place in Knoxville when Tim played a big Tennessee player whose temper was about as bad as Tim's. They played a long three-setter that Tim won 7-5 in the third. On numerous occasions their arguments on calls almost resulted in fisticuffs. After the match one of my players told me he had heard that this Tennessee player, who was a heavyweight in size and larger than Tim (a well-built 165-pounder), planned to "jump" Tim when he came out of our locker room.

I knew that Tim would not duck a fight, but I was concerned that he might break his right hand, which is easy to do in bare-knuckle brawls. So I quickly looked up Coach Louis Royal of Tennessee and told him what I had heard, adding that Delaney was a former Golden Gloves boxing champion in the tough Washington, D.C., area and had once killed an opponent in the ring (a slight exaggeration). I made it clear that if they got into a fight somebody was sure to get hurt, and that my advice was for Coach Royal to get his player out of sight when we boarded our van. I guess my advice was heeded because when Tim came out of our locker room to board our van, Coach Royal and his battler were nowhere to be seen.

Postscript: once on the van headed for our next match against Kentucky in Lexington, I told Tim what had transpired, and — I should have known it — he got mad as hell at me for not letting him "whip up" on the Tennessee player.

OF MONKEYS, DONKEYS,
AND YANKEES

In 1982 Lindsey Hopkins, Jr., approached me with an inter-esting proposition:

"Dan," he said, "Coca-Cola would like for you to go over to Beijing and spend several weeks teaching modern tennis techniques to the Chinese professional coaches. They really haven't been able to do much in tennis since the early 1930s."

My first inclination was to politely refuse this kind of offer. I had not quite yet gotten over the jet lag from my trip to Tokyo for the collegiate all-star matches against Japan five years earlier. But Mr. Hopkins had been too good to me and the University of Georgia for me to turn down any request of his.

So I agreed, and in August it was my pleasure to spend three weeks in Beijing, working with 40 Chinese instructors from various provinces. Accompanying me was my Georgia assistant coach and former All-America player Bill Rogers. The trip was co-sponsored by the All-China Sports Federation and Coca-Cola Export, and our Chinese hosts literally "killed" us with kindness.

We spent our last few days at a seaside resort city, Bei Dai He, northeast of Beijing, a five-hour train trip. There we observed China's national championships for men and women, also the juniors.

One of the highlights of the trip was twice playing doubles with the distinguished vice premier of China, Mr. Wan Li, who also was the honorary chairman of the China Tennis Association. In our first match, my partner (one of the Chinese instructors) and I defeated Mr. Wan and another instructor, and I vividly recall that my partner was terribly embarrassed by being a party to the vice premier's defeat.

The next day we played again, and this time Mr. Wan had as his partner the former national doubles champion of China. But Mr. Wan really didn't need a better partner because this time my partner missed every shot he tried. It seemed to me that he was making certain that he didn't "disgrace himself," a lowly tennis instructor, by again being party to the defeat of the vice premier.

The vice premier chatted with me at length about what China could do to be stronger in tennis. I told him I saw no reason why China could not become a tennis power if it simply put special emphasis on a sound training program. But the first thing China had to do, I said, was build more tennis courts. I pointed out that we had more tennis courts in little Athens, Ga., than he did in all of Beijing, a city of some eight million people.

We had a wonderful young Chinese woman who acted as our interpreter. Li Li was her name, a 22-year-old graduate of the University of Beijing. One evening, as Miss Li Li and I were walking in downtown Beijing, I told her that I could not tell the difference between Chinese, Japanese and Vietnamese people. She replied, with a smile, that she could not distinguish between monkey, donkey and yankee.

I quickly explained that I was from the Southern part of the United States, and that we had fought the yankees from up North and that her joke did not apply to me, but that it was certainly apropos for a real yankee.

DEANE FREY
AND THE "DEAD BALL TRICK"

Deane Frey, a fine prospect from Lynchburg, Va., made an immediate impact at Georgia. As a freshman in 1982 the hard-hitting baseliner with the two-fisted backhand won the Conference Indoors No. 5 singles and No. 3 doubles with Tom Foster. He never failed to win an SEC Indoor singles crown the next three years (No. 3 in 1983 and '84 and No. 4 in 1985). He helped us win four straight SEC Indoor team titles and two SEC Outdoor crowns, not to mention starring on the 1985 NCAA championship team.

This Virginian is remembered for many contributions to Georgia's tennis success, but perhaps the most unforgettable incident of his distinguished career occurred in the SEC Outdoor championships, which actually finished up indoors because of rain in our own Lindsey Hopkins Indoor building.

Deane was playing Tennessee's Earl Grainger, a South African, in the finals of No. 4. Grainger led, 5-3, in the third set, serving with the game score tied two-all (no-ad scoring). At this point Grainger served, and the ball did not bounce at all, causing Frey to whiff the ball completely. Well, Deane just went out of his mind. He picked up the "dead ball" and knocked it high in the air all the way down to Court 1. Chair umpire Dr. George Pirie, in turn, immediately awarded a penalty point to Grainger, and since Grainger had reached match point on Frey's whiff, the penalty point ended the match.

Frey, needless to say, was almost foaming at the mouth after getting the "abuse of ball" penalty. He charged the umpire's chair, objecting profusely and profanely. By the time I had noticed the bedlam on court No. 4 and dashed down there, Deane was speaking in an unknown tongue, and it took a little while for me to learn what had happened. Then I told Deane that all he had to do was pick up the "dead ball," which probably had busted on contact with the court, and show it to the umpire, who would automatically rule the point be replayed. But Deane, still frothing at the mouth, retorted: "But it was not our match ball that was served; it was a worn-out, beat-up ball at least two years old."

The bottom line was, as I explained to Deane, he should

not have hit the dead ball down to court No. 1; he should have produced it as evidence to the umpire.

To which Deane replied, "The bottom line is that I have been royally rooked."

"ALLEZ, MON PETIT!"

Mikael Pernfors, Georgia's illustrious two-time NCAA champion, joined the pro tour in 1986, and I frequently talked to him on the phone, mainly to keep up with him and to wish him good luck.

At the French Open that year, when he upset his fellow countryman Stefan Edberg in the second round in a tremendous five-set match, I got so excited I called him immediately.

"Surely do wish I were with you," I said, after offering my congratulations.

To which he retorted, "What's stopping you?"

I never once thought about going to Paris, but suddenly it dawned on me that I ought to go, "seize the moment." Why not? I had grown up on Georgia red clay courts, and the French Open was the granddaddy of all red clay tennis championships. I had some work that needed finishing, but I told Mikael that if he was still in the tournament June 4, I'd be there. "Who do you play next?" I asked him.

He told me that he would next meet Robert Seguso, the former Southern Illinois-Edwardsville star (later to win the Wimbledon doubles with Ken Flach), and if he got by Seguso he probably would play the talented clay-court specialist from Argentina, Martin Jaite.

Mikael did indeed defeat Seguso and Jaite, so I hopped on a plane with two fellow Athenians, former Georgia tennis player Dick Budd and his wife Ginky. Ginky and Dick are probably Athens' greatest tennis aficionados, and both are tremendous supporters of our tennis program. Furthermore, they laugh at my jokes, so I was happy to be with them.

We arrived in the City of Light just a few hours before Mikael's quarterfinal match with none other than the reigning Wimbledon champion, the big redhead, Boris Becker. By reaching the quarters, Mikael was entitled to box seats for his friends; so the Budds and I, along with former Georgia NCAA doubles champion Ola Malmqvist (Mikael's coach/manager) and Richard Howell of Atlanta (Mikael's agent) all sat together.

Becker was the No. 3 seed, behind former French Open champions Ivan Lendl and Mats Wilander. When Becker won the first set from Mikael, 6-2, I turned to Ola and lamented, "I see Mikael is wearing Nike shoes. When did he change from Adidas [which he'd been wearing the last three years]?"

Ola replied, "This morning. He just signed a big contract with Nike."

"That's a mistake," I said, "switching shoes in the middle of a tournament. It takes time to get used to a new brand of shoes."

When Mikael won the next set, 6-4, I said to Ola, "Thank God! He's finally broken those damned shoes in!"

Mikael went on to win the next two sets, 6-3, 6-0, and we all were ready for a big celebration at one of those famous French restaurants that evening. Mikael joined us, and he especially enjoyed an incident that took place: a handsome French couple sitting in a booth next to us, unable to ignore our frivolity and merrymaking, suddenly approached our table.

The gentleman said to me, "Sir, my friend and I have been listening to your accent, and we have a wager on what part of England you are from."

Well, Mikael nearly fell out of his seat laughing, and he answered the question before I could, saying, "He's not from England at all. He's from the Southern part of the United

States where a lot of people down there talk that way."

A few minutes later the head waiter delivered to us a fine bottle of French champagne, compliments of our new friends from Paris.

Two nights later we were celebrating Mikael's great semi-final victory over the French idol Henri LeConte, 2-6, 7-5, 7-6, 6-3, and my son, Ham (excited by watching Mikael beat Becker on television) had flown over from Athens to join us. But in the finals, Ivan Lendl — at the peak of his great career — was too tough for Mikael, winning 6-3, 6-2, 6-4, in a two-and-one-half-hour battle much closer than the scores.

Still, it was an unforgettable few days in Paris, especially because Mikael's play all week had completely won the hearts of the fun-loving French fans. Perhaps bored by the methodical play of such previous champs as Bjorn Borg, Mats Wilander, and Lendl, they really cheered for the diminutive and lovable Swede. I'll always remember their wonderful rallying cry: *"Allez, mon petit!"*

By the way, Mikael's superb showing in Paris helped him win professional tennis's Rookie-of-the-Year award and also vaulted him to the No. 10 ranking in the world. His career since then has been hampered by a series of injuries, yet his indomitable fighting spirit has enabled him to return and *twice* win the Comeback-Player-of-the-Year award.

AL PARKER, THE ALL-VICTORIOUS VALEDICTORIAN

Back in the summer of 1978 I saw a boy, nine years old, win the 10-and-under singles title in the Crackerland championships at the University of Georgia's Henry Feild Stadium. He had the blondest head of hair I ever saw — cut in the Prince Valiant pageboy style.

After presenting him his trophy I told him that he had the talent to go a long way in tennis, and I added that I hoped one day he would be wearing the colors of his state university in Athens. We shook hands and he gave his trophy to his proud parents, Mid and Sally Parker, who were standing by.

I never saw Al Parker play tennis again until the fall of 1987 — nine years later — when he entered the University of Georgia as a freshman on a tennis scholarship. I did, however, write him quite a few congratulatory letters during that nine-year span. The first one was when he captured the USTA Boys' 12 singles and doubles. He went on to win the USTA singles and doubles crowns in the boys' 14, 16 and 18 age groups, and also to rank No. 1 in all four age divisions — the first and only player ever to do so. He won 25 USTA national junior titles — 12 in singles, 13 in doubles — a record that stands today.

Needless to say, every major tennis school in the country tried to get him. He only visited a few campuses, his own state university being one of them. When he told me that he had made up his mind and that his choice was the University of Georgia, I hollered, "Thank the Lord Almighty! I have never sweated out such a decision by a tennis player in all my life."

Al replied with a smile, "I don't know why you were worried, Coach. Back in 1978 when you told me you wanted me to play for Georgia some day, we shook hands, and that sealed the deal as far as I was concerned. You owed me a scholarship whether I was worth a damn or not."

Time flies, and Al Parker's four years at Georgia went by terribly fast. But I think his collegiate career was even more amazing than his fabulous junior career. Despite a multitude of injuries, including a back injury as a freshman that caused some doctors to say he would never play tennis again and a stress leg fracture and rotator cuff shoulder injury as a junior, he nevertheless earned All-America honors four straight

"All-victorious" Al Parker

years.

He twice won the Southeastern Conference round-robin No. 1 singles, twice won the Southern Collegiate singles and thrice won the doubles of this tough event. He twice won the Volvo All-America national collegiate singles, and three times he led Georgia to the SEC team tournament finals.

Time and time again, when he should have been sidelined nursing an injury, he displayed physical courage and a loyalty to his team that went above and beyond the call of duty.

There are four so-called Grand Slam titles in collegiate tennis; in 1991 there were four different winners. Al Parker of Georgia won the Volvo, Patricio Arnold of Georgia won the

DuPont Clay Courts, Conny Falk of Miami won the Rolex Indoors, and Jared Palmer of Stanford won the NCAAs. In head-to-head competition against each other, Al Parker beat them all. For that conclusive reason, the Intercollegiate Tennis Coaches Association named Al Parker its Player of the Year.

Al Parker always has been a teetotaler and he religiously observed all Georgia's training rules — except one. Frequently he was guilty of burning the midnight oil — staying up late, well past midnight: *studying . . . doing his lessons!* As a result, he frequently was too tired to play well the next day. But all was not in vain. His senior year in 1991 he was presented with the following awards:

- the Southeastern Conference's Boyd McWhorter Scholar-Athlete-of-the-Year Award;
- the University of Georgia President's Award to the Outstanding Senior Student, honoring Al for his perfect grade point average of 4.0 during his entire college career;
- and the NCAA's Award to the Scholar-Athlete-of-the-Year in all sports.

Imagine being named the nation's outstanding performer in a sport and also being named the outstanding student-athlete in all collegiate sports! Al Parker did it. I doubt we'll see his likes again!

Unfortunately, injuries continued to plague Al during his brief fling in professional tennis, but he did win a few USTA satellite circuit tournaments before deciding to enter business. He certainly ought to be a whopping big success, having graduated from the University of Georgia's Business School at the head of his class in finance — not to mention being valedictorian of the senior class.

While Al has brought great credit to his hometown, the most famous citizen of little Claxton (population 2,694) is actually another Al Parker, the genius who made the Claxton Fruit Cake world renowned. Grandfather Parker was a good athlete himself — a star quarterback at Claxton High — and was offered a scholarship from Auburn. He had to turn it down because he needed a job at the bakery to help his family during the terrible Depression days of the 1930s. His oldest son, Middleton Albert Parker, known as "Mid," was a five-letter athlete in high school and at college, Georgia Southern in nearby Statesboro. Mid was named for his mother, the former Delorease Middleton of Long County, Ga., whose name is one of the most illustrious in Southern history (Arthur Middleton of Charleston signed the Declaration of Independence).

Mid Parker was a good student, too, certainly smart enough to marry the beautiful Sally Edwards of Claxton, who graduated *magna cum laude* at Georgia Southern. She had been valedictorian of her class at Claxton High, following in the footsteps of her father Tom Edwards. So when her son, Al Jr., graduated valedictorian at Pinewood Christian Academy in Claxton he became a third generation valedictorian.

No wonder Al Parker, Jr., became the "all-victorious valedictorian."

BILLY LENOIR,
TWO-HANDED PHENOMENON

I was 34 years old when I began coaching Georgia's tennis team in 1955, but I had actually "coached" the young boys of Athens in the late 1930s and early 1940s while I was in college and was managing Georgia's six red clay courts. I didn't know much about tennis in those days, but several of those Athens boys went on to become No. 1 players in college — despite my "coaching."

I had counted on being Georgia's No. 1 player my senior

season of 1942, but the war came and Georgia canceled its minor sports program. I didn't get to play much tennis in the Marine Corps (the Marines didn't 'go in' for tennis), nor did I have time to play tennis while working three and a half years on the *Atlanta Journal* sports staff. But in the summer of 1950, after having returned to Athens in September 1949 to join Georgia's athletic staff, I resumed my own tennis playing career at age 29 after an eight-year layoff.

That summer of 1950 I met one of the finest boys I have ever known: Billy Lenoir. His dad, Professor James Lenoir of the Georgia Law school, asked me to help Billy with his tennis when Billy was about eight years old. Prof. Lenoir gave Billy his own racquet, which was much too big and heavy for Billy to swing with one hand. So Billy used both hands on both his forehand and his backhand shots. Eventually, he became the best boy player in town. But I told Billy he would never go far hitting the ball with two hands — the belief held by most of the coaches and teaching pros in those days.

So Billy — to please me — tried to hit with one hand. He practiced hard. When he was 15 years old, in the finals of the Southern Boys' at Davidson, N.C., he tried to win with one-handed shots and got behind. He asked if he could return to his two-handed style, and I acquiesced. Billy began hitting those wonderful two-handed shots and went on to victory. After that match I told Billy to forget about one-handed shots and to just go ahead and "do his thing."

Three years later Billy "did his thing" and won the National Boys' 18 singles at Kalamazoo, Mich., defeating Dennis Ralston in the semis and Frank Froehling in the finals; he also won the coveted Tom Stowe Award for being the best sportsman and competitor there.

I guess the proudest I've ever been at a tennis tournament was at Kalamazoo that summer of 1960 when Billy upset the great Ralston (who earlier that summer had won the Wimbledon doubles at age 18) in the semifinals. At the same

Junior champions Ham Magill (l) and Billy Lenoir

time that Billy was playing Ralston, on the court immediately adjacent to them was a Boys' 15 semifinal match between the No. 1 seed, Mike Belkin of Miami Beach, Fla., and my son, Ham. Belkin won a long match from the back court on red clay (they have hard courts at Kalamazoo now), 3-6, 6-4, 6-4. It was the only set Belkin lost in three years of boys' play, and he won the finals the next day without losing a game.

During those semifinal matches, I was sitting with Frank Willett of Atlanta, the former Georgia Tech star who was president of the Southern Tennis Association at that time, and we were both as proud as peacocks.

If either Billy or Ham had played on my Georgia teams, we would have been strong enough to have won the SEC team title in the 1960s, quite a few years before we finally "broke the ice" in 1971 with another hometown boy leading us: Danny Birchmore. But Billy left Athens when he was 16, along with his family, for Phoenix, Arizona. His older brother Carter had asthma, and it was necessary for him to move to the Arizona climate. Dr. Lenoir got a position as law professor at the University of Arizona, where Billy made All-America three straight years for Coach David Snyder (who later compiled an outstanding coaching record at his alma mater, the University of Texas).

Ham went to Princeton University where he also made a fine record. He was a member of the crack Tiger team in 1964 that ended Miami's record dual match winning streak at 137 straight, and as a senior he played No. 1 for the Tigers, his best win being at Coral Gables against Miami's brilliant Jaime Fillol.

On the Distaff Side of the Net

THE BEAUTIFUL BARBARA DuPREE

In the summers of the early 1950s, I used to give tennis tips to the children of several friends — one of whom was the beautiful raven-haired daughter of Georgia's backfield coach, Sterling DuPree. Barbara DuPree was about 11 years old when I began teaching her on our old red clay courts, and I was still helping her in 1958 when the varsity complex was moved to its present location.

Barbara had inherited wonderful athletic ability from her dad (a great football player and track man at Auburn), and she quickly developed into one of the top players in the South. I think she made the biggest improvement in her game during the spring and summer of 1958 when she was 18, about to enroll at Georgia. The reason for the jump in her game was the rivalry that developed between her and her daily sparring partner, my son Ham, who ranked No. 1 in the Southern Boys' 13 singles.

Barbara and Ham were good friends and often helped their dads pick muscadines during home wine-making days.

Barbara DuPree with her daughter Julie Moran.

Their rivalry intensified because their dads, whenever Barbara and Ham played, would sit at opposite ends of the old bleachers aside Court 1 and spur them on. That is, whenever Barbara switched sides and walked by her dad, he would whisper, "You can't let a little kid beat you." And whenever Ham walked by me, I would whisper, "Don't you dare let a girl beat you." Following such exhortations,

Barbara and Ham would fight their hearts out, usually playing long 9-7 and 10-8 sets.

Late that summer both Ham and Barbara beat everything in sight in the Crackerland championships. Ham won the boys' 13 and boys' 15 divisions, and Barbara won both the girls' 18 singles and, with a stunning upset over state women's champion Betty Jo Braselton of Atlanta, the women's open singles as well.

In college Barbara gradually quit playing competitive tennis since Georgia didn't have a women's team in those days. She had to settle for being a campus beauty queen and earning a Phi Beta Kappa key.

However, the DuPree athletic prowess and interest in sports has continued through the third generation. Barbara's daughter Julie Bryan was an accomplished equestrian growing up in Thomasville, Ga., which is real horse country, and she also played basketball and tennis on her high school teams. And like her mother, Julie too is a beauty; as a teenager she won the National Junior Miss title, and today she is one of the most beautiful women in television, doing an outstanding job as a sports commentator with NBC Sports. She is, of course, the famous Julie Moran.

BECKY BIRCHMORE, "MEN'S" TENNIS TEAM MEMBER

When the Wickliffe twins Billie and Jo used to play on Georgia's varsity courts in the 1950s, I told people (including those in charge of women's activities at UGA) that it was a shame colleges did not have intercollegiate athletics for women. And a few years later I was still trying to get the university to form a women's tennis team when my protégé Barbara DuPree was state champion.

Finally, in the early 1960s the SEC took its first steps toward permitting women to play intercollegiate sports. All the women had to do was to be good enough to make the existing men's varsity teams, the thinking being that a university had one team to represent the school and the members of the team whoever excelled at that sport — men or women. A very few women did make some of the golf, swimming and tennis teams, not many as regulars but a few as substitutes. Alabama had a women's tennis player good enough to be a regular: Roberta Allison, the National Intercollegiate Women's champion. (At the time, though, this championship wasn't sponsored by the colleges, but by the United States Tennis Association; the women joined the NCAA in 1982.)

In 1963 we had a hometown girl certainly good enough to play as a substitute on our team: Becky Birchmore, state women's champion, a remarkable girl and the daughter of the inimitable Fred Birchmore, who was a champion boxer at Georgia and later internationally renowned for riding his bicycle around the world in the 1930s. Fred named his bike Bucephalus for Alexander the Great's famous warhorse, and it stood next to Lindbergh's Spirit of St. Louis in the Smithsonian Institute when I visited there in 1941.

Fred married his college sweetheart, the former Wiladean Stuckey of Brunswick, Ga., and they had four children, all good tennis players and all good students. Fred used to quip, "They got their brains from their mother, an accounting major at Georgia who never made a mistake until she married me."

Becky was the oldest child, followed by Fred Jr., Linda and Danny, one of the finest tennis players in the history of the SEC (All-America in 1971 and 1972).

I was delighted when women were ruled eligible to play for SEC "men's" tennis teams in 1963, Becky's senior year at Georgia. She had learned to play tennis on our courts and frequently had played members of our men's team in practice. Since she was popular with our men players (and also since her dad daily dragged and rolled our clay courts for exercise), we didn't have any problems at all when she made the eight-"man" squad. She played No. 8 and was a substitute in four matches that spring. I do think she might have played as a regular on several lesser teams in the SEC, but we finished as runner-up in the SEC tournament and had a strong team: Charley Gaston, Carleton Fuller, Chuck Harris, Pierre Howard, Charles Benedict and Mack Crenshaw, Jr., with Anthony Arnold as first sub and Becky as the second sub. Becky actually was undefeated, winning three doubles matches (Sewanee, Mercer and Emory) and one singles match (Emory).

Becky Birchmore

Becky earned a B.S. degree, a Master's degree in medical microbiology, a law degree and finally a degree in medicine. Now married and mother of three children, she is a patent lawyer for the Japanese company Sheshido and commutes to offices in Tokyo, Detroit and Boston. She also is a visiting professor at Harvard where she lectures on dermatology.

Being the first female varsity tennis player at the University of Georgia was merely a stepping stone in an illustrious career for Becky Birchmore, truly a "Wonder Woman."

LISA SPAIN,
A TRUE GEORGIA PEACH

One of my favorite Georgia tennis players was lovely Lisa Spain, the NCAA singles champion in 1984 — a charming and vivacious, dark-haired South Georgia girl from Moultrie.

I fell in love with Lisa the first time I saw her, which was in 1973 when she came up to Athens and played in our Crackerland junior championships. She was only 10 and she lost in the age 12 singles quarterfinals to Jaime Kaplan of Macon (later a star at Florida State) 6-0, 6-1. Afterwards, I tried to pick up her spirits (her uncle Frank Spain was a big Georgia football supporter and longtime friend of mine) by telling her she had the talent to be a champion. She returned to Athens the next three years and won her division each time.

I was not surprised when Lisa went on to win the Georgia High School Class AAAA singles crown four straight years, and I was delighted when Georgia women's coach—and my prize protégé—Greg McGarity (now associate athletic director at the University of Florida) informed me that Lisa would enter Georgia on a scholarship in September 1980.

In her freshman season at Georgia, Lisa was runner-up in the Southeastern Conference No. 1 singles, which she later won in both her junior and senior years.

In the fall of Lisa's senior season (October 1983) she won the ITCA All-America singles at Myrtle Beach, S.C., and in May at UCLA she won the coveted NCAA singles, defeating Stanford's outstanding Linda Gates in the finals, 7-5, 3-6, 6-2.

Lisa Spain holds her NCAA singles champion trophy.

She also nipped Trinity's brilliant Gretchen Rush in a torrid three-set semifinal battle, 3-6, 7-6 (12-10), 6-3.

The same day, a few hours earlier, Georgia's Mikael Pernfors had won the NCAA men's singles in Athens. In fact, Lisa telephoned the Georgia clubhouse to see how Mikael had fared; the match had just ended, and she was able to congratulate Mikael himself. Several hours later Mikael reciprocated by reaching Lisa in her Los Angeles hotel room to congratulate her for her great victory.

Lisa's best shot was a powerful, looped forehand drive, with which she controlled play. She also had a strong serve, and she was a good smart athlete with plenty of fighting spirit.

Lisa tried professional tennis for a while (Kenny Rogers had been impressed by her and sponsored her pro career), and she even won several matches at Wimbledon, but she wanted to marry her hometown and college sweetheart, Georgia law school graduate Herbert Short. So she quit the circuit, settled down in Atlanta, and taught tennis at the Atlanta Athletic Club until her family got too big (three children as of this date).

I'm looking forward to the day when she returns to where it all started — the Crackerland Championships — and collects a few more trophies.

SHANNAN MCCARTHY — CLOSE TO A TRIPLE CROWN

Another of my favorite Georgia players was a beautiful blonde, Shannan McCarthy, who almost won three national collegiate singles titles during her sparkling four-year Georgia career: 1989 through '92. She and her identical twin, Shawn (a fine player, too), were born in Athens when their parents were students at the University of Georgia. She grew up in Atlanta but won her first tennis trophy in Athens when she was only nine years old: she and Shawn were finalists in the girls' 12 doubles at the 1979 Crackerland.

Ten years later Shannan and Shawn were back in Athens as freshman stars at Georgia. Shannan was an especially good athlete, with great speed afoot; she was an agile, strong, very aggressive player, especially dangerous at the net. She very quickly made a name for herself; her fine play earned her national collegiate rookie-of-the-year recognition.

As a junior she lost in the finals of the ITA National Clay Court singles to Julie Exum of Duke, 6-1, 2-6, 6-2, and she also lost in the finals of the ITA Rolex National Indoors to Nicole Arendt of Florida, 3-6, 7-6, 6-4. She later avenged both losses in dual matches the same season.

Shannan had a fantastic senior season in 1992, twice beating Florida's Lisa Raymond in dual matches, but unfortunately she bowed to the superb Gator star in the NCAA finals, 6-3, 6-3.

Shannan in her senior year set some records that still stand. She was 33-2 in singles, once winning 32 matches in a row. Her four-year total of 36 matches won in Collegiate Grand Slam events ties her with Sandra Birch of Stanford for the all-time record for a male or female player.

GEORGIA WOMEN SWEEP IN 1994

In June of 1981, a few days after the NCAA men's championships in Athens, I received a letter from Jeff Wallace, who had played two years for Utah's fine coach Harry James. A native of Oregon, Jeff had played in the NCAAs in Athens twice, and he was so impressed by the enthusiastic crowds and exciting atmosphere that he wrote me he wanted to be a part of it.

I didn't know Jeff at all, but I had a high regard for his coach, and I immediately phoned Harry James about Jeff's letter. Harry told me he was aware of it and that he would okay Jeff's desire to transfer to Georgia. Furthermore, he wished Jeff the best of luck and told me that Jeff would make us a valuable player.

Jeff was ineligible his first year in Athens because of the transfer rule, but he played regularly in 1983 and 1984. He was captain of the 1984 team, winning the No. 6 singles in the SEC tournament, and he won a key match for us in the quarter-finals of the NCAA team tournament over Antony Emerson (son of Australia's world champion Roy Emerson) that helped us upset top-seeded Southern California, 5-4.

Two years later Jeff asked me to recommend him for the vacated position of head coach of Georgia's women's team. I gave him my strongest recommendation, and he was hired. He has done a terrific job, twice being named national Coach of the Year, and his teams have twice reached the final round of the NCAA team tournament, losing to Stanford in 1987 and defeating The Cardinal in 1994.

Jeff's 1994 Georgia team was one of the most powerful in collegiate annals. It won both the USTA-ITA National Indoor and NCAA (Outdoor) team championships. Its "big gun" was senior Angela Lettiere of Vero Beach, Fla., who had made All-America as a freshman but was handicapped by a bad knee both her sophomore and junior years. Finally healthy again as a senior, Angela made a spectacular showing in the four collegiate Grand Slam singles events: semi-finalist in the Clay Courts, finalist in the All-America, finalist in the Rolex Indoors and winner of the NCAAs — defeating Keri Phebus of UCLA, 7-6, 6-2. In addition, she and freshman Michelle Anderson of South Africa, though they missed the NCAAs because of an injury to Anderson, nevertheless finished the season ranked No. 1 in the nation; they had won the Rolex National Indoor doubles.

In the 1994 NCAA team tournament Georgia defeated Southern California, 5-2; Duke, 5-0; California-Berkeley, 5-3, and perennial champion Stanford, 5-4, in a four-hour finals that The Cardinal coach Frank Brennan called "the best college match I have seen."

With the team score tied at 4-4, Georgia finally clinched the match and championship by winning the No. 2 doubles. Stacy Sheppard and Tina Samara beat Beth Berris and Kristine Kurth, 6-1, 7-5. I was particularly pleased that Stacy, a native of nearby Loganville, Ga., hit a backhand winner on match point. Eleven years earlier, on the same courts, Stacy had won my Crackerland age 10 singles. I remember it well because Stacy's big Prince racquet was almost larger than she.

Tips on Tournaments, Draw Sheets & Team Line-Ups

DIRECTING A TOURNAMENT

I have been running off tennis tournaments for so many years that I've probably run off more than any other person in the country. For example, in 1988 I ran off the Southern Senior Men's Indoors in January, Georgia State Collegiates in April, NCAAs in May, Crackerland Juniors and Adults in July, Athens City Juniors and Adults in August, Southern Collegiates in October, ITCA Region Three Indoors in November, and Georgia State Open Senior Men's Indoors in December.

The first tournament I directed was the Athens City in the summer of 1938 when I was 17 and managing Georgia's old red clay courts. From 1938 through 1941 (up until World War II) I annually ran off the City and Crackerland championships. From 1942 through 1949 I took an eight-year leave of absence, while serving in the Marine Corps during the war and then working four years on the *Atlanta Journal* sports staff. But I resumed directing the same tournaments in the summer of 1950, having joined Georgia's Athletic staff in

September 1949. And when I became Georgia's coach in 1955, I gradually began running off more tournaments, even originating some of them — like the Georgia State Collegiates and the Southern Collegiates.

Counting the four years before World War II and the 45 years since 1950, I have had the opportunity to learn much about running off tennis tournaments. First and foremost, the tournament director must realize that he has a tremendous amount of work to do himself and must delegate considerable other work; then he must ensure it is done and done right. This is part of my checklist, not necessarily in order of importance:

THE COURTS must be shipshape. There's nothing worse for the players than having to perform on hard courts that are cracked and need to be resurfaced. The courts should be clean, frequently hosed down with a power nozzle. College tennis is almost exclusively played on hard-surfaced courts now, but if the courts are clay, they will require much more work to be in shape for all-day tournament play. When I managed Georgia's old red clay courts in high school and college days during the summertime, I'd ride my bike to the courts early every morning, water them down with a hose, wait a while and then drag them, roll them, line them with wet lime, and then admiringly scrutinize them. There is nothing prettier than a freshly-worked red clay court.

NETS AND CENTER STRAPS must be in good shape. Patch up any holes in the nets or, preferably, get new nets. Check on the center straps to see if they are slipping, which old ones will do.

SINGLES STICKS should be painted every year. It's wise to put a mark on each court designating where the singles sticks should be placed — 36 inches from the outside of the singles alley toward the net post.

CHAIRS OR BENCHES should be placed on the courts for the players and coaches to use during the switch-over.

WATER CONTAINERS AND PAPER CUPS should be on all courts.

SCOREBOARDS should be on each court by the umpire's chair, to be operated by either the umpire or the players. Scoreboards are a must in order to get and keep fan interest. The best scoreboards were originally designed in 1972 by Coach Stan Drobac of Michigan State. They have large numerals and spaces for three sets, and they can be read from both sides.

UMPIRE CHAIRS should be high enough for the ump to have a commanding view of the full court, and they should be comfortable (some matches last a long time). An umbrella for the ump ought to be installed too.

DARK CURTAINS OR SCREENS should be at both ends of the playing court. Players must have a dark background in order to keep the ball in focus.

THE GRANDSTAND must be in order and kept clean at all times. It is necessary to have an attendant or several helpers to keep the courts and entire tournament area clean throughout the day. There should be a small trash can on each court, and larger ones at appropriate places throughout the site.

TOURNAMENT HEADQUARTERS should be easily accessible to the players and officials, and clearly marked. It should be equipped with at least one telephone, preferably two, and a public address system. There should be telephones at other sites for the public's and players' use.

BULLETIN BOARDS for draw sheets and pertinent tournament announcements should be at several spots — and kept up to date.

DRESSING ROOM FACILITIES, SHOWER ROOMS AND TOILETS should be available for the players, coaches and officials. There also should be rest rooms for the fans, and they must be kept clean throughout the day.

A TRAINING ROOM should be available for the trainers,

at least one of whom should be on duty at all times. Trainers also have the responsibility to supply the players with drinks, ice and towels at courtside.

A DOCTOR, at least one, should be either on hand or available (quickly) at all times. Also, ambulances must be available.

CERTIFIED USTA UMPIRES AND LINESMEN must be at all collegiate matches nowadays. It is the tournament director's duty to get well-trained ball boys/girls for certain matches, especially the later rounds.

PUBLICITY (newspapers, radio and television) is absolutely vital to get good attendance at matches. In college play, both the coach and sports information director must cultivate good media relations and "sell" the sports media on the attractiveness of tennis and its popularity in the community. There must be both advance publicity and follow-up coverage of the matches.

TICKET SALES PROMOTION should be started well in advance for tournaments and big matches.

Committees can be formed to handle most of these details. The team's most enthusiastic fans should be the core of the support group from which committee members can be selected. They can be both men and women, young and old (a mixture is ideal, I think). In the many years we have run off the NCAA championships at Georgia we have been fortunate to have had a magnificent support group of volunteers, many of whom have helped for over 20 years. We have had an especially wonderful group of ladies who have helped as ushers, program sellers, and concession workers, as well as offering transportation (and good old Southern hospitality) to players and VIPS.

The tournament director by all means must have several reliable and experienced troubleshooters at standby. He must have an electrician and plumber on call at all times, also police. And certainly not least, he ought to know the latest weather situation at all times.

In short, he's got to have all the bases covered.

MAKING THE DRAW

Although I had played in a few tennis tournaments, I knew nothing at all about how to officially make the draw when I "directed" that first Athens City tournament back in 1938. Fortunately, the top authority in town on such matters was a good friend, Dr. Milton P. (Big Mit) Jarnagin, and he taught me the rudiments by simply interpreting a USTA rule book that he owned.

Dr. Jarnagin had played tennis at UGA, and he became very much interested in the game when he read mathematics at Oxford, at which time he attended several Wimbledons. Dr. Jarnagin also was our No. 1 umpire in town, often making pronouncements with a fake British accent which he and all of us enjoyed.

Making the draw is an important (and sometimes complex) affair. There is the official way listed in the USTA Yearbook, showing where to place the seeds and the byes, and how to draw the names out of a hat — all of which was explained to me by Dr. Jarnagin. He was a stickler for making the draw "by the book," but later on I learned that making a draw by the book was not always the best or fairest way, nor the best way to have a popular, successful tournament. Modifications must be made for various types of tournaments.

In college tourneys, we frequently place players from the same school in different quarters, which makes sense and is fair. There's no need for a player to face his teammate in the first round. In the NCAA championships we go a step further; we try to prevent players from the same geographic

Athens' first tennis umpire, Dr. Milton (Big Mit) Jarnagin.

region from clashing in the first round.

Naturally, in USTA championships one should go by the USTA rules, but in our Athens City and Crackerland sectional tournaments we have special guidelines in making the draw. I have learned that it makes a player mad as hell when he comes 100 miles or more to Athens and learns his opponent in the first round is his buddy from home with whom he has been practicing every day. It also makes him mad when he draws his doubles partner as his first opponent, or if he draws the same person he played in the first round the previous year, or if he draws the top seed for the second or third straight year.

In such tournaments, of course, I make the seeding officially but I try to solve these problems by throwing the player's name back in the hat and drawing again. So I'm still drawing everything "out of the hat" — *officially* by the book (my book).

To seed players appropriately, the draw-maker should gather all the seeding information possible: previous year's rankings and current tournament results. I'm also a firm believer in seeding and placing as many players as possible, once again covering all the bases. There are a lot of players who think they should have been seeded, and when they complain to me I always say, "My good fellow, you WERE seeded — actually PLACED in the draw, RIGHT THERE." I point to the spot, which satisfies most complainers because most of them don't even know where a seeded or placed player should be in the draw, anyway.

Making the draw is a thankless job, too. In the senior tournaments in which I play and also direct, a lot of my fellow seniors tease me (or accuse me) by saying I put all the tough players in the half of the draw opposite me. Then, if I should happen to win the tournament, they claim my final opponent was so tired from having to play all the tough players that he didn't have anything left against me in the finals.

ESTABLISHING THE LINE-UP

Establishing his or her line-up is a vitally important part of a tennis coach's job. The coach's system must be eminently fair to the players, all of whom aspire to play as high on the line-up as possible. All candidates must have equal opportunity to earn position. Otherwise, the coach will have legitimate complaints not only from the players but also from their parents, who are important in the total picture because they certainly exercise influence on their sons an ddaughters. It would be impossible to have the necessary "esprit de corps" if a player were not given a fair chance to gain his rightful place.

In my 34 years as coach at Georgia I used several systems to derive the line-up. Occasionally, I played it "by ear." It is a mistake to have a hard and fast rule. There is such a thing as the coach's prerogative, but it must not be abused.

I recall a funny story (funny now, anyway) involving my own tragic experience in a challenge match when I was a player at Georgia. I was on both the swimming and tennis teams, and the swimming season in those days did not end until April, by which time our tennis season was half over. Nevertheless, our coach (Howell Hollis, Georgia's freshman football coach and a good friend of mine) let me challenge for a position, starting at the bottom. I beat the Nos. 7, 6 and 5 men and then was ready to take on the No. 4 man. If I could beat him, Coach Hollis was going to let me join the four-man team going to the conference tournament at Vanderbilt. I prevailed in a long match, but got terrible blisters on my hands and feet, which were soft from so much swimming. But I figured I had a couple of days to recover before leaving for Nashville.

The next day, Coach Hollis said to me, "Dan, you ought to play Paul another challenge match. He's done a good job for us all season, and you should play a best-of-three match series."

I told him about my bad blisters and asked for a day or two to get well, but coach Hollis said we simply didn't have time to wait a couple of days. We played that very afternoon. I couldn't even hold the racquet, much less run, and got the pants beat off me.

Coach Hollis comes up and says, "Dan, you can play it off tomorrow."

I knew my blisters would be even worse then, and I was so mad and frustrated that I went up to the blackboard by Court 1, which was used for our scoreboard in matches, and hit it with my right hand as hard as I could. I had done some intramural boxing, and it was the best right cross I ever threw. It knocked the everlasting crap out of the scoreboard — and also broke my hand. It was many moons before I played tennis again.

When I first began coaching, I myself played our boys every afternoon, at least one set with two players, sometimes with three of them. I learned all their strengths and weaknesses, and I thought I could rank them perfectly at positions one through six. If I had any doubts, I would have those particular players clash in challenge matches.

The best thing about that system was that it got me in good shape for my own tournaments. I really improved my game. But eventually I learned (I was not a fast learner) that I could do a better job by observing the boys play each other on two or three courts at a time. I could coach more players that way.

After those early days when our season was limited to the spring quarter of school, I began using the challenge match system exclusively to determine the line-up. We were now playing year-round and had plenty of time in the fall to play our challenge matches, and the weather was good too. At first, we had the candidates play a single round-robin, but eventually we expanded to a double round-robin that generally lasted until late February.

The double round-robin was eminently fair, but it was hard on the players, who often get more uptight for challenge matches than they do for regular dual matches and tournaments. Later, as we began playing more fall tournaments and didn't have the time for a double round-robin, I added more criteria: results of tournament play and past play on our team.

There is no doubt that challenge matches are a hassle. I call them "necessary evils." Some boys, especially players who have not played tough challenge matches in high school, at first cannot play their best in challenge matches. It might take them a year or two before they are mentally tough enough to play as well in challenge matches as in a dual or tournament match.

Once we had a fine boy, a very good player, who was so unnerved by our challenge match system that his parents came over and discussed the matter with me. They wanted me to abandon our challenge match system and to select the line-up based on my judgement of a player's ability and potential. I told the parents that I appreciated their feelings, but I wanted their son to fight his way out of his phobia about challenge matches. Fortunately, the boy did fight his way out, and he became our No. 1 player and made All-America. Several years later he wrote me a letter of appreciation for "making a man" out of him. Needless to say, I saved his letter for future use and have pulled it out several times.

Another time I had an irate mother telephone me. "Coach Magill," she said, "you have been terribly unfair to my son. He has beaten everybody on your team in challenge matches, yet you have him playing down at No. 6! How can you explain this injustice?"

"Well, Mrs. So-and-so," I said, "I can explain it very easily. It's true that your son did play all the other players on the team, but he gave you a somewhat erroneous report on the outcome of his matches. He did not win any of his challenge matches. He lost all of them."

"You don't say so," the startled mother stammered. "That beats all. When he comes home, I am going to have his father speak to him!"

"Damned good idea," I said.

I kept a record of all our challenge matches, and, after finalizing the line-up, I would give the players a copy of all the results of their challenge matches, dual matches, and tournament matches that I used as criteria in making the line-up. I also would mail a copy of it to the player's parents, and sometimes to the boy's hometown pro.

The two biggest weaknesses of the challenge match system are, first, that they often make the players too uptight; and, second, that sometimes a lower-ranked player, with nothing to lose, can play over his head and upset a better player who is a bit too tight. But the strength of this system is that it gives all candidates a shot at each other for a team position, and it toughens up the players if it doesn't kill them off first.

And after all, the coach is looking for the survival of the fittest, those who are mentally tough.

There were only two players I ever excused from taking part in challenge matches: Danny Birchmore in 1972, and Mikael Pernfors in 1985. Both were in their senior years. Danny had won the SEC No. 1 singles the previous year and Mikael had captured the NCAA singles the previous year. I talked it over with the other team members, all of whom agreed that Danny and Mikael deserved to be excused.

By the way, in my early years of coaching there was a great deal of so-called "stacking" the line-up. There were no specific rules against it, and frequently a coach brazenly put his worst player at No. 1 if he thought his regular No. 1 man had no chance against the opposing team's ace. Finally, our SEC coaches worked up a system that would eliminate this practice. The solution was to prohibit players from moving up or down more than one position from one match to another. In the NCAA Team Tournament nowadays a school must use the same line-up every match unless a player is injured. In addition, a special committee of coaches scrutinizes the line-ups when first submitted, looking for any possible irregularities.

How Athens, Georgia, Became the Mecca of College Tennis

The University of Georgia's first tennis courts were built at the turn of the century: four dirt courts near the entrance to the campus, parallel to Broad Street in downtown Athens. Those courts were ploughed under around 1930 and replaced with the greensward still prevalent today. New red clay courts were built adjacent to the university's old basketball arena, and they served students, faculty, staff, and the varsity teams through 1950.

In 1951 Georgia Coach Albert Jones, with the help of President Jonathan Rogers, came up with funds to build two "strictly varsity" courts in a beautifully wooded spot right above the south side of Sanford Stadium, the university's football field. These courts were "rubico," a so-called "clay court" actually made of finely crushed rock and colored light green. A couple of years later two more courts were added, making a fine four-court layout with a small grandstand aside Court 1.

That was the layout I inherited when I succeeded Coach Jones, my longtime friend, in 1955. But in the summer I learned that a tremendous new Science Center was to be built with a new physics building right on the site of the courts; I also knew that the Athletic Association was in bad financial straits at the time and probably wouldn't be willing to spend a dime for new courts. Fortunately, the university had laid aside funds to replace the courts they were commandeering for the Science Center.

I was delighted with the proposed site for the new courts — an undeveloped end of the South Campus — and I seized the opportunity to design a two-tiered layout, with three upper courts and three lower ones (thereby finagling the two additional courts we badly needed).

In March of 1958 we dedicated six new rubico courts, accompanied by a small, one-room clubhouse and a little wooden grandstand aside Court 1. Our new facility didn't look like much that first year, but it had possibilities. I knew the Athletic Association wasn't going to spend a penny to develop the area, so I began planting dogwoods and redbud seedlings.

When Henry Feild, our No. 1 player in the mid-sixties, died in an auto accident in 1968, his parents, Professor and Mrs. D. Meade Feild, donated the money to add another room to our clubhouse, which was subsequently named for Henry. We later put a little roofed pavilion on top of the clubhouse for VIP seating.

In 1968 we replaced our dirt courts with asphalt-based hard-surfaced courts; we were the last in the SEC to do so. I hated to change from my beloved dirt courts, but we were handicapped playing in SEC tournaments on courts so much faster than we were used to.

When the NCAA decided in 1977 to make Georgia the permanent site of the NCAA men's championships, Georgia Athletic Director Joel Eaves was so pleased that he authorized the construction of an imposing metal grandstand on the hill overlooking the upper three courts. The completed stadium, too, was dedicated to Henry Feild.

The responsibility of annually putting on the NCAAs made me determined to further develop our facility into one truly worthy of hosting the world's premier amateur tennis tournament. I got permission from Athletic Director Eaves to call on former lettermen and friends for financial help in this enterprise.

In 1980 one of my own greatest dreams was realized when the University of Georgia built four indoor courts adjacent to our outdoor courts. Our benefactor was the great American sportsman and Georgia alumnus Lindsey Hopkins, Jr., whose

Georgia's "new" varsity courts, 1958.

oldest son, Lindsey Hopkins III, was an outstanding player at Georgia and the captain of my 1959 team.

There are some interesting sidelights in the history of our indoor courts. The contractors unexpectedly found underground water and tons of rock on the site of the proposed building, causing the costs to almost double the original estimate — which was also the amount of Mr. Hopkins' donation.

I wasn't about to go back to Mr. Hopkins to bail us out, but I did get Athletic Director Joel Eaves' permission to ask President Fred Davidson for help. Fortunately, President Davidson thought it would be a bargain for the University to get four indoor courts and have to pay for less than half the costs, so he made up the difference with Athletic Association funds.

Because the University did not build the indoor courts with state funds, I was told that the electric bill and upkeep of the indoor building would be *my* responsibility! Even though the Hopkins Indoor building was the only building on the campus not maintained by the University or Athletic Association and the only indoor tennis facility on any campus in the United States (according to my inquiries) not maintained by its college, I agreed to assume the responsibility of meeting the necessary expenses. Surely this is one for Ripley's "Believe It or Not." But such was my commitment to tennis and my belief that we had to have indoor courts. The Athletic Association now assumes responsibility for the upkeep of the Hopkins Indoor building, but to this day, every morning I turn in to the Association the receipts collected by attendants for indoors play by the faculty, staff, etc., and personally see to it that we stay "in the black."

Our indoor facility has been embellished through the years by the generosity of former Georgia tennis lettermen Pierre Howard, Jr., Dick Budd of Athens, Lindsey Hopkins III and Martin Kilpatrick, Jr., of Atlanta. Metal bleachers seating 1,000 fans give it the largest seating capacity of any college indoor tennis layout in the country, and we've also added an air-conditioning fan, a dressing room/shower, and a tournament headquarters office.

The Lindsey Hopkins Indoor building has been a major reason for Georgia's success in tennis, both men's and women's. It has been the site of many indoor tournaments, including the SEC Indoors on several occasions. Many times it has been the battleground of the ITA Region Three

Lindsey Hopkins, Jr., with Bill Hartman and David Benjamin.

Collegiate Indoors and the Georgia State Senior Men's Indoors held annually in December during the Christmas holidays. And, of course, during inclement weather Georgia dual matches and NCAA championship matches are played there, enabling us to keep these crucial events on schedule.

In October 1960 I accompanied a beautiful Athens girl on a plane trip to Los Angeles: Marianne Gordon. She had worked part-time for me in the athletic office and was also a friend of my own children.

My trip was brief, but Marianne stayed a little longer. She was destined for show business and became a fixture on the long-running "Hee Haw," where she was always featured as the Southern belle in a long white dress, usually sitting in a swing on the ol' plantation house veranda. While she was at it, she married country music star Kenny Rogers.

The couple returned to Marianne's hometown, where Kenny built a magnificent home for her on a palatial estate near Athens. At that time Kenny had just become interested in tennis himself, and one day Marianne brought Kenny to the UGA tennis courts to meet me. Kenny played doubles on our courts with Athenian Woody Chastain, former Georgia baseball player whose sister Edwina (now married to Tom Johnson, head of CNN) was a lifelong friend of Marianne. They had been classmates growing up in Athens and also friends in California when Tom Johnson was editor and publisher of the *Los Angeles Times*.

A few days after meeting Kenny, Woody called to tell me that Kenny, who had helped UCLA's tennis program when he lived in Los Angeles, wanted to do something to help Georgia's program.

"What can he do?" asked Woody.

It so happened that the Intercollegiate Tennis Coaches' Association wanted to locate its Collegiate Tennis Hall of Fame at Georgia's Henry Feild Stadium because we were hosting the NCAAs every year and the coaches simply figured that Georgia was the ideal site for the Hall of Fame.

So I told Woody, "We're trying to get funds to build the Collegiate Tennis Hall of Fame adjacent Henry Feild Stadium. Could Kenny help finance this project?"

Woody told me to call Kenny and talk it over with him, and I did so that very day. Kenny suggested that I work up the plans and estimated costs and then get back in touch with him.

In May 1984 we dedicated a handsome new building, the home of the Collegiate Tennis Hall of Fame, with Kenny and Marianne and their son Christopher Cody Rogers all taking part in the ceremonies before a big crowd on hand for the NCAA championships.

And what a wonderful addition to our facilities the Hall of Fame has proved to be — a fascinating repository of collegiate tennis history and memorabilia.

Enshrined here are photos of all Hall of Fame members; photos of all winners of national tournaments sponsored by the Intercollegiate Coaches Association; and photos of all past winners of the Rafael Osuna Award, the Ted Farnsworth Award and the Wilson Coach of the Year Award.

Another display pays tribute to some of the greatest teams in collegiate annals: George Toley's Southern California team of 1963; Glenn Bassett's UCLA team of 1971; Dick Gould's 1978 Stanford team; among others.

And there's an impressive mural of the members of the first U.S. Davis Cup team; former Harvard stars Dwight Davis (whose idea it was to have an international competition), Holcombe Ward and Malcolm Whitman — all of whom were national collegiate champions. This trio defeated Great Britain in the inaugural Davis Cup match in 1900.

Mounted next to the mural, and of special historic value, are the racquets used by this first Davis Cup team: the Spalding Oval and the Spalding Vantage — 95-year-old replicas donated to us by the late Norman Holmes, Sr., longtime Melbourne, Fla., teaching pro and father of Georgia All-American Norman Holmes, Jr.

In fact, there are more than 100 racquets on display in the Hall, including several sent in by Tony Trabert and one of the Wilson T2000s Jimmy Connors used to win Wimbledon. (By the way, the wooden racquet I'm holding on the jacket photo for this book was the last wooden racquet to win the NCAA singles championship — used by Utah's Greg Holmes in 1983.)

There are good stories behind many of our acquisitions. For example, one of the Hall's big fans and supporters is Hunter Lott of Bryn Mawr, Pa., a former star at Pennsylvania. (He and his wife, by the way, donated a beautiful watercolor of the Merion Cricket Club, where the collegiate championships were held from 1900 to 1934.) On one

Marianne Rogers and Stan Smith at Hall of Fame induction ceremonies.

of his visits to Athens, Mr. Lott pointed out that his alma mater had produced quite a few NCAA champions, but none were pictured in the Hall. I explained that I had repeatedly requested the pictures from the University of Pennsylvania but had never received a reply. Well, within 48 hours I received a special delivery packet from Pennsylvania with every missing picture — including a rare photo of Big Bill Tilden himself the only year he attended college, as a freshman at Penn in 1914.

I later learned that Mr. Lott, one of Penn's most prominent alumni, had "suggested" to those in charge that they rush the missing photos.

Another good story concerns Valentine Hall, Columbia's doubles champion in 1988 with Oliver Campbell.

Columbia's sports information office sent me Campbell's picture but could not find one of Hall. However, the vice president of the school told me that he thought Hall was a relative of Eleanor Roosevelt and that I should check with the Roosevelt Archives at Hyde Park. Sure enough, they had one of Mr. Hall in later life and sent it right to me. There's little doubt he was kin to Eleanor; there is a striking resemblance.

By the way, Kenny often returned to our courts and especially loved to play in the Celebrity Doubles event during the annual Hall of Fame induction ceremonies, always held during the NCAA men's championships. On several occasions he won this event, teaming with the great American player Dennis Ralston, then coaching Southern Methodist University.

Celebrity Doubles: (l-r) Vic Seixas and Andy Johnson lost to Kenny Rogers and Dennis Ralston.

In one of these Celebrity Doubles matches, Kenny and Dennis, with the connivance of baseball immortal Hank Aaron, pulled a joke on the great Gardnar Mulloy (winner of more titles than any American player in history, counting senior events). Gardnar was one of the greatest competitors who ever lived, and he particularly wanted to win this match against Kenny and Dennis.

On their match point, Dennis (as prearranged) hit an easy serve to Hank who smacked the ball higher than any tennis ball I have ever seen hit. Swinging with two hands, exactly like he hit a baseball, he sent it soaring high over the Hall of Fame building, and as he hit the ball, the stadium P.A. announcer (whom I had alerted) said, "Number 756 — a new record for Hammerin' Hank Aaron!" The big crowd cheered loudly; but guess what an incensed Gardnar Mulloy did? He demanded that the point be replayed. Another sidelight: the ball landed right on top of Coach Vince Dooley's head; he was walking across the parking lot to say hello to Hank, a fellow townsman of Mobile, Ala.

A wonderful part of the Hall of Fame building is its balcony, which includes 200 excellent box seats overlooking the three stadium courts. We have gradually added more box seats, forming an impressive quadrangle. Our box-seat addition above the clubhouse alongside Court 1 was named for Joe Heldmann, a promising Georgia freshman in 1983 who lost his life in an auto accident in Mexico City. His parents, Anton and Elfriede Heldmann of Warren, N.J., donated the money for this improvement.

Then, in 1986, in commemoration of our 1985 NCAA team championship, our lettermen provided funds to build box seats with a beautiful canopy between our upper and lower courts. A few years later, when longtime friend and supporter Dr. Robert West died, this pavilion was named in his honor.

"Big allowances" were made for (l-r) Lindsey Hopkins III, Richard Courts II, and Alfred Thompson, Jr.

The two-deck building behind Court 4, which serves as headquarters for our many tournaments, was donated by staunch supporters Dick and Ginky Budd of Athens.

Athletic Director Vince Dooley generously appropriated funds to build much-needed men's and women's rest rooms for the fans, a training room and shower for the players, a players' lounge and a media room (all constructed beneath the main grandstand). The lounge was named in honor of the late Joe Heldmann, and the media room was named the Manderson Room in memory of the late Ed Manderson, Jr., and his twin brother, Joe, team captain in 1962. Ed and Joe have generously supported their alma mater's tennis program.

Alfred Thompson, Jr., a top-notch player in the late '50s,

has been one of our leading financial contributors. He gave the electronic scoreboard and the double-decked eatery so popular during the NCAAs when the university's food services cater meals for the fans.

Incidentally, when Alfred played, there were two other Atlanta Piedmont Driving Club boys on our team, Lindsey Hopkins III, and Richard Courts II, all protégés of famed teaching pro Jack Waters. They also were the sons of prominent Georgia alumni, three of the state's wealthiest citizens: Alfred Thompson, Sr., one of the owners of Life Insurance Company of Georgia; Lindsey Hopkins, Jr., the No. 2 stockholder in Coca-Cola; and Malon Courts, head of the South's largest investment company, Courts and Company. These Atlanta "Buckhead boys" each had an allowance greater than Georgia's tennis budget; and when we traveled to out-of-town matches, they loudly denounced the meager meal tickets allowed each player (usually fast food) and the tight motel accommodations (usually four to a room). However, they must have really liked "roughing it" because none of them ever spent one dime of their own money to upgrade the situation — even though I encouraged them to do so just to stop their griping. (All have been very generous since their graduation, I should add.)

Another Athens girl, another beauty, and another who reached stardom in Hollywood was also instrumental in the development of our world-class facility — Kim Basinger. And like my association with Marianne Rogers, my friendship with Kim began many years ago when she was just a teenager.

It all began in the late '60s and early '70s when Kim used to visit Henry Feild Stadium along with sisters Ashley and Barbara to watch their dad Don and brother Mick play in Athens City and Crackerland tournaments. One summer I asked Kim to manage my drink stand during the tournaments, and I do believe we had the most sales ever when she was behind the counter.

In the summer of 1990, after she had attained fame and fortune as a model and actress, Kim was in town to visit her family and she came out to the courts one day to watch her nephews (Mick's boys Brantley and Kelly) play in the Crackerland Boys' tournament. Afterward, Kim came by tournament headquarters to see me; she was dressed very casually with her mane of hair pulled back under a hat, no makeup, and dark glasses perched on her nose. And if you can believe, *I did not recognize Kim Basinger.*

"Coach Magill," she said, "You all surely have made a beautiful place out here. I wouldn't recognize it from the way it looked when I ran your drink stand. How did you manage to make such a transformation?"

Immediately I dropped everything I was doing and took Kim on a tour, explaining how we had acquired our facilities: "Alfred Thompson gave us the big electronic scoreboard; Lindsey Hopkins gave us the indoor building; Marianne and Kenny Rogers gave us the Collegiate Hall of Fame building," and so forth. Naturally, I also told Kim how proud we were of *her* success in Hollywood.

A few days later her brother Mick called to say that Kim was so impressed with our tennis setup, she wanted to know how she might further improve it. I told Mick that the NCAA Tennis Committee wanted us to put in championship lights so that we could play night matches in the NCAA tournament.

"Kim will donate the lights," said Mick.

As a result of Kim's interest and generosity Henry Feild Stadium now has lights similar to those at the U.S. Tennis Center in Flushing Meadows, N.Y., generally considered the best in the world.

Kim joined us for the dedication ceremonies April 10, 1991, in a match between Georgia and West Virginia. Kim

Kim Basinger turned on the lights in 1991 (with Pierre Howard in the background).

looked like a million dollars, dressed in the prettiest white ensemble I ever saw, and at the conclusion of her remarks she yelled to the big crowd, "GO DAWGS!" which brought down the house. Then she walked over to Georgia star Al Parker and surprised and embarrassed the heck out of him by planting a big kiss on his cheek.

I guess you could say she lit up Henry Feild Stadium. And by the way, both the NCAA semifinal and final team tournament matches were played under the lights in 1993.

Recent improvements include additional box seats alongside Court 1, funded by lettermen and dedicated to the late Leighton Ballew, longtime head of the university's drama department, and to Charles Hooper, a tennis letterman from the '20s; a splendid air-conditioned press box atop the stadium funded by the Athletic Association; and — especially dear to my heart — the many different species of native American azaleas that now abound throughout the grounds, donated by Cason Callaway, Jr., of Callaway Gardens.

There's always more to do, but these wonderful additions and improvements — thanks to the generous support of so many loyal alumni and friends — truly have made Athens, Ga., the mecca of college tennis.

Canopies, box seats, grandstands and lights make Henry Feild Stadium the mecca of college tennis.

CHAPTER 10

A History of the NCAAs in Athens

THE NCAA CHAMPIONSHIP FINDS A HOME

It's still amazing to think that the National Collegiate Athletic Association (NCAA) tennis tournament, the very oldest of championships in American collegiate sports, found a home in little Athens, Ga., when it was held for the first time on the University of Georgia campus June 12–17, 1972.

It was a huge success, so much so that the chairman of the NCAA Tennis Committee, Dale Lewis of the University of Miami (Coral Gables), said he wanted Athens and UGA to become the permanent home of the NCAAs just as Omaha is the home of the NCAA baseball "College World Series."

Everything went like clockwork: perfect weather six straight days, fantastic publicity in the Athens and Atlanta newspapers in particular, magnificent "Southern hospitality" by the hometown hosts, record daily crowds of 2,000 to 3,000 cheering fans who were privileged to see one of the best fields ever to play in the NCAAs.

There were umpires in the chair for every match (singles and doubles) for the first time in the tournament's long history. The dean of American umpires, Mike Blanchard himself, was on hand. There also were big scoreboards on each court — another first. And the draw was the largest in the tournament's annals: 184 in singles, 86 teams in doubles, requiring 268 matches to be played in six days on 14 adjacent outdoor hard-surfaced courts. There were no indoor courts then nor any lighted courts. Fortunately, God was on our side. It didn't rain a drop that week, but it rained day and night the next week.

The 88th Annual NCAAs came to Athens as part of the geographic rotation plan that began in the late 1930s. Originally, the national collegiate tennis championships (known simply as "the intercollegiates" until World War II) were conducted under the auspices of the United States Lawn Tennis Association (USLTA). The first one was held in Connecticut — not at venerable old Yale University but at the state insane asylum's recreation courts in Hartford in 1883, and again there in 1884. Then it moved to the New Haven Lawn Club in 1885 and was held there through 1899. In 1900 it moved to the famed grass courts of the Merion Cricket Club in Haverford, Pa., just outside Philadelphia (a hotbed of American tennis from the very beginning).

USLTA officials (including many of the early collegiate champions from the Ivy League schools that pioneered tennis and all other collegiate sports in this country) thoroughly enjoyed running off "the intercollegiates," and the event flourished on the grass amongst the "blue-blood" society at Merion every year from 1900 through 1934 (except the World War I years of 1917–18).

However, in the 1930s more and more colleges began hiring bona fide tennis coaches. Most of the coaches up to this time were faculty members who "coached" without pay and spent most of their time, naturally, doing what they were paid to do: teach. They coached the tennis team for the love of the game, and it was a hobby for them — though many of them had played college tennis themselves and were eminently capable of teaching tennis for a living.

Nevertheless, the so-called "professional" collegiate coaches did two things in 1934: First, they decided that, since virtually all collegiate matches were played on either clay or hard-surfaced courts, the national collegiate championships should not be held on grass. Second, they decided to rotate the championships from one part of the country to another.

So in 1935 "the intercollegiates" left Merion and moved westward to the clay courts at Northwestern University in Evanston, Ill. (Northwestern's professional coach Paul Bennett was a leading advocate of the new changes.) The tournament did return to Merion from 1937 through 1941, but was held on clay courts there instead of grass.

Then the tournament began being held all over the country: in the South for the first time in 1942 at Tulane University in New Orleans, then back to Northwestern, and finally to the Pacific coast for the first time, in both 1947 and 1948 at UCLA under the direction of Coach Bill Ackerman, the "father" of Bruin tennis.

From 1949 through 1971 it moved to the campuses of Texas, Northwestern again, Syracuse, University of Washington, University of North Carolina, Kalamazoo College, Utah, U.S. Naval Academy, Northwestern again, Washington again, Iowa State University, Stanford, Princeton, Michigan State, UCLA again, Miami in Coral Gables, Southern Illinois (Carbondale), Trinity (San Antonio) Princeton again, Utah again and the University of Notre Dame in 1971.

Miami's Hall of Fame Coach Dale Lewis was responsible for the NCAAs being in Athens in 1972. He had been impressed by the big crowds Georgia had been drawing for major matches, especially against longtime national power Miami. Well over 3,000 fans had attended a showdown between Georgia and Miami in April 1972 when the

Hurricane snapped Georgia's consecutive home winning streak of 76 dual matches. Miami's Eddie Dibbs trimmed Georgia's pride, Danny Birchmore, a hometown product, in a spectacular three-set battle at No. 1 singles.

Informed people knew that the University of Georgia was the nation's oldest state-chartered institution of learning: founded in 1785 (four years before George Washington became president of the United States). Now informed people also know that the University of Georgia is the "home" of the oldest national intercollegiate athletic championships: tennis, since 1883.

ATHENS' FIRST NCAA, 1972

Little Trinity University of San Antonio (under veteran coach Clarence Mabry) and Stanford University (under up-and-coming young Dick Gould) dominated the historic first NCAAs in Athens in June 1972.

For the first time in 13 years, the USC-UCLA stranglehold on the team title was snapped by Mabry's men, who had been knocking at the door the previous two years, being runner-up to UCLA in both 1970 and 1971. Mabry was a native Texan who had been a star player and protégé of the legendary Dr. Daniel Penick at the University of Texas in Austin. He had assembled a powerful team, built around two New Yorkers, Dick Stockton and Paul Gerken; Brian Gottfried of Florida and Bobby McKinley of St. Louis, Mo., the younger brother of Wimbledon champion Chuck McKinley, who also had played for Mabry at Trinity.

Stockton and Gottfried provided an All-Trinity finals in the singles, with Stockton winning a hard-fought battle, 4-6, 6-4, 6-3, 6-2.

The state of Georgia's immortal Bitsy Grant of Atlanta

provided a bit of color by umpiring the singles finals. Bitsy himself had been a collegiate star at North Carolina, NCAA finalist in 1931, and also a member of the victorious United States Davis Cup team in 1937.

Some of the tournament's best tennis was played in the singles semifinals. Stockton edged Stanford's Roscoe Tanner, a native Southerner from nearby Chattanooga who had been

Trinity's 1972 team champions: (l-r) Dick Stockton, Coach Clarence Mabry, Paul Gerken, Bobby McKinley, Brian Gottfried.

a finalist the two previous years, in a furious five-setter; and Gottfried trimmed Stanford's Sandy Mayer in the other bracket (Mayer won the title the next year).

The losing singles semifinalists, however, came back to win the doubles diadem. Mayer and Tanner upset the No. 1 seeds, Stockton and McKinley in the semis, and then toppled Gottfried and Gerkin in the finals, 6-1, 3-6, 6-3, 6-4 for the

Stanford's 1972 doubles champions Sandy Mayer and Roscoe Tanner with Coach Dick Gould.

first of many NCAA titles to be captured by the protégés of Stanford coach Dick Gould.

The overall field really was one of the most distinguished ever assembled for collegiate play. Five went on to win professional Grand Slam titles: Tanner won the 1977 Australian singles and in 1979 he was runner-up to Bjorn Borg in a memorable five-set Wimbledon finals; Mayer won the 1975 Wimbledon doubles and 1979 French doubles; Gottfried and Raul Ramirez of Mexico (Southern California) won the French doubles together in 1975 and 1977, and Wimbledon doubles in 1976; and Freddie McNair (North Carolina) won the French doubles in 1976.

And two of host Georgia's greatest players ever were impressive: senior Danny Birchmore extended the hard-serving Tanner in a round of 16 featured match; and freshman Manuel Diaz of San Juan (later to make All-America and become the Bulldogs' highly successful coach) won two matches before bowing to UCLA ace Jeff Austin, brother of the outstanding women's player Tracy Austin.

That historic first NCAAs in Athens set a standard of excellence for future hosts, including Georgia, that has been hard to equal.

THE FIRST TEAM
TOURNAMENT, 1977

The year 1977 marked several important milestones in the long history of the NCAA tennis championships:

First, the tournament returned to Georgia, as the coaches had promised following the successful 1972 NCAAs in Athens. But its return had to be delayed because of the long-range geographic schedule that sent it to Princeton in 1973, Southern California in 1974 and Corpus Christi in 1975 and 1976.

Second, Henry Feild Stadium had a huge new grandstand, seating 3,100. (Additional box seats built since then now bring the total capacity to 4,000.) The new grandstand reflected the appreciation of Georgia Athletic Director Joel Eaves for the NCAA's plans to make Georgia a regular site of the championships, and Coach Eaves also was pleased that

Georgia teams had won the Southeastern Conference tournament six of the previous seven years.

Third, since Corpus Christi had made a slight profit for the first time in NCAA tennis history, the NCAA in 1977 asked Georgia to make a financial guarantee of $15,000. Georgia Athletic Director Eaves told me he was doubtful that we could net $15,000 and he seemed reluctant to gamble that we could do it. So I said that the Athens Tennis Association, which I had helped form in 1950 to finance the annual Athens City and Crackerland summer tournaments, would take that responsibility. It still does, and the guarantee in recent years has soared to $100,000.

Fourth, the team tournament was introduced to the NCAA format. Previously, the team champion had been determined by counting matches won in the individual singles and doubles tournaments, and the coaches had argued that system did not decide a true team champion. Finally, in 1977, the NCAA Tennis Committee prevailed upon the NCAA Executive Committee to let us experiment with a team tournament, which Michigan State coach Stan Drobac had first brought into being in 1973 when he talked the ITCA (the coaches' association) into hosting a national team indoor tournament at the University of Wisconsin in Madison.

The team tournament was an immediate success and has become the most exciting part of the present NCAA championship format. The team tournament is played first, followed by the individual singles and doubles tournaments that have been going on since 1883. This new format had the nation's top 16 teams in the team tournament, with the top 64 singles players and top 32 doubles teams in the individual tournaments. The selection process had the country divided into eight geographic regions with each region sending its best team, its four best singles players and two best doubles teams; the other half of the field was selected at large.

Dynamic Dick Gould piloted Stanford to victory in the

inaugural team tournament, an event his men were to win 10 of the next 16 years as he compiled one of the greatest coaching records ever by a coach in any sport.

Stanford defeated Utah, California-Berkeley, UCLA and Trinity in succession. In the finals against Trinity, coached by young Bobby McKinley who had been a star on Clarence Mabry's victorious Trinity team in Athens in 1972, the six singles matches were split, but The Cardinal won No. 1 and No. 3 doubles to clinch a thrilling battle, 5-4.

Matt Mitchell, a quick all-court player with a great volley, led Stanford to the team title, winning all four of his matches at No. 1 singles and also all of his No. 1 doubles matches with partner Perry Wright.

Top-seeded Mitchell maintained his fine form in the ensuing singles tournament, defeating in succession John Bennett of Brigham Young, John Austin of UCLA, Ben McKown of Trinity, Bruce Nichols of UCLA in a thrilling three-setter (4-6, 7-6, 7-6), Chris Lewis of USC in the semis and Tony Graham of UCLA in the finals (6-4,1-6,6-3,6-4). Graham was seeded only No. 12 but upset No. 2 Bruce Manson of USC in the semis (6-4,7-6), after having almost fallen to Georgia's net-rushing Charlie Ellis in the quarters in a very close three-setter (6-1, 3-6, 6-4).

Mitchell and Wright were seeded No. 1 in the doubles but were toppled in the quarters by UCLA's unseeded pair of John Austin and Bruce Nichols, who in turn upset their No. 8 seeded teammates Ferdi Taygan (later to win the French Open doubles) and Van Winitsky in the semis; Austin and Nichols went on to lose to USC's No. 5 seeded tandem of Bruce Manson and Chris Lewis in the finals (6-2, 6-3, 6-7, 6-3).

All in all, the tournament was a big success, despite some rain that forced several matches to be played on temporary cement courts on the floor of Georgia's basketball coliseum. (Georgia built four championship indoor courts in 1980, which have been a big help in recent NCAA tour-

Stanford's Matt Mitchell, the 1977 singles champion.

naments during inclement weather.)

The NCAA Tennis Committee unanimously and enthusiastically scheduled the championships to return to Athens in 1978, a ritual that would take place 13 straight years.

THE GREATEST NCAA FINALS
OF MODERN TIMES

The most exciting NCAA men's singles finals of modern times was the four-hour battle of the Johns, McEnroe of Stanford and Sadri of North Carolina State, in 1978 on the University of Georgia's fast-playing hard-surfaced courts.

The fast courts helped the powerful Sadri, a six-two senior with the hardest serve in college tennis. Seeded only 11, his booming serve had earned him an upset win over the No. 2 seed, backcourt specialist Eliot Teltscher of UCLA in the quarterfinals, 6-1, 7-6, and also another stunning victory over the No. 3 seed, South African Eddie Edwards of Pepperdine in the semi-finals, 6-1, 6-7, 6-1.

McEnroe was perhaps the most heralded freshman in NCAA history, having reached the semifinals of the Wimbledon men's singles the previous year at age 18. When I saw him play for the first time (three months earlier as he led Stanford to the ITCA National Indoor team tournament crown at Madison, Wis.), I wrote that he was the most gifted U.S. shotmaker I had seen since Big Bill Tilden (generally considered the greatest player of the first 50 years of tennis history).

But McEnroe did not have an easy time making it to the final round against Sadri. Undoubtedly he was bothered by a strained back muscle he had pulled in leading Stanford to the team tournament championship earlier in the week, and he had spent many hours in Georgia's training room getting treatment. He was extended to three sets in both his quarter-

The incomparable John McEnroe.

final and semifinal matches, nipping Trinity's talented Erick Iskersky, 6-2, 6-7, 6-1, and his own teammate big Bill Maze, 6-4, 6-7, 6-2.

On this hot May day McEnroe was determined to end his collegiate career by capturing the oldest national championship of American collegiate sports. Both McEnroe and Sadri planned to turn professional following this match.

The big crowd of 3,000-plus fans, most of whom were pulling against McEnroe because his temper tantrums during previous matches had annoyed them, was treated to tennis at its most exciting. The epic struggle lasted four hours and 25 minutes, with the fiery redhead from New York City winning, 7-6 (5-3), 7-6 (5-3), 5-7, 7-6 (5-3). Jimmy Van Alen's no-ad scoring system, with its "sudden death" best-of-nine-point tie-breaker, further added to the drama.

Although McEnroe won three of the four sets, he won only one more game overall than Sadri, 26 to 25, and the total points each player won were dead even: 144 points apiece.

Sadri served 24 aces, which averaged six aces per set. McEnroe served only three aces, but I thought his serve was just as effective as the obviously more powerful Sadri's. McEnroe was cunningly deceptive in placing his southpaw slices and topspins, mixing them up as he beat a tattoo on the corners of the service boxes. He also demonstrated the masterful net game that later was to win him eight Wimbledon crowns (three in singles, five in doubles) and eight U.S. Open titles (four in singles, four in doubles).

Besides the fantastic McEnroe-Sadri match, the '78 NCAAs will also be remembered for the great Stanford team that ran roughshod over a very tough field in the team tournament.

Dick Gould has said his '78 team was the best he ever coached, which makes it one of the strongest in NCAA history. The presence of the mighty McEnroe alone, although only a freshman, made Stanford stronger than The Cardinal team that won the previous year. But there was another talented

Big-serving John Sadri.

freshman, also a lefthander and native New Yorker: Peter Rennert. And there were four returning stars: defending NCAA singles champion Matt Mitchell (who played only No. 3 on the 1978 powerhouse), big Bill Maze, John Rast and Lloyd Bourne.

This star-studded juggernaut pulverized South Carolina, 8-1; Arizona State, 8-1, and the No. 4 seeds, Southern Methodist, 7-2, in the semifinals, "clinching" in the singles every day.

In the finals, though, Glenn Bassett's No. 2 seeded UCLA Bruins extended their intrastate rivals to a 6-3 decision. Stanford won the singles, 4-2, but was extended to three sets in two matches they barely won: Matt Mitchell over Tony Graham at No. 3, Peter Rennert over Bruce Nichols at No. 4. In the feature match between the nation's No. 1 and No. 2 ranked players, McEnroe trimmed Eliot Teltscher, 6-4, 7-5.

Early in the doubles, however, McEnroe and Mitchell (the NCAA singles champions of 1978 and 1977) triumphed at

No. 1 over John Austin and Teltscher, 6-1, 7-6, to provide Coach Gould with his fourth NCAA team crown in six years.

The individual doubles tournament was won by the UCLA team of John Austin and Bruce Nichols, who had been runners-up to USC's Bruce Manson and Chris Lewis the previous year. Although only seeded third, they were not to be denied. They beat the No. 2 seeds, Matt Mitchell and Perry Wright of Stanford in the semis, 3-6, 6-3, 6-4; and the No. 4 seeds, Kevin Curren and Gary Plock of Texas in the finals, 6-4, 6-4, 6-2 (finals were the best of five sets then). Curren and Plock had knocked off the No. 1 seeds, McEnroe and Bill Maze in the semis, 6-2, 6-4.

John Austin, the younger brother of former UCLA star Jeff Austin, two years later won the Wimbledon mixed doubles with sister Tracy Austin; Curren in 1982 won the U.S. Open doubles with Steve Denton and the Wimbledon mixed doubles with Anne Smith.

The 1978 NCAAs in Athens left the fans in a "can't wait" mood for 1979.

KEVIN CURREN REIGNS IN '79

Kevin Curren, a tall, gangling South African with a powerful serve, not only upheld his No. 1 seeding in winning the 1979 NCAA singles, but he also became the first player in four decades to go through the always rugged field without losing a set. The only other player to accomplish this fantastic feat in the past 41 years was Tulane's Ham Richardson in 1953 at Syracuse University.

Curren became the third Texas Longhorn to win the coveted NCAA crown, following in the footsteps of the immortal Wilmer Allison (1927) and Berkeley Bell (1929). Incidentally, Curren's coach, Dave Snyder, played for Wilmer Allison when

Kevin Curren, the 1979 singles champion.

the former Wimbledon champion tutored the Longhorns.

It was the great South African player Cliff Drysdale, now famous as a TV tennis commentator for ESPN, who recommended to Curren that he play collegiate tennis in the United States before turning professional. Six years later — in 1985 — Drysdale must have been very proud, indeed, when Curren defeated both John McEnroe and Jimmy Connors en route to the finals at Wimbledon, where he lost a tough four-setter to Boris Becker.

In winning the 1979 NCAA singles, Curren notched straight-set victories over David Geatz, New Mexico; Tony Giammalva, Trinity; Marty Davis, California-Berkeley; Arjun Fernando, SIU-Edwardsville; No. 3 Fritz Buehning, UCLA, in the semis; and Erick Iskersky of Trinity in the best-of-five set finals, 6-2, 6-2, 6-3.

Iskersky was certainly one of the best players never to win the NCAAs. He won the National Collegiate Indoor singles

Francis Tarkenton (r) awards the '79 team trophy to UCLA's Glenn Bassett.

in both 1979 and 1980, and also had beaten Curren four of the five times they played (Curren had won their last meeting, though).

Iskersky and Trinity teammate Ben McKown won the doubles, one of the few times the crown has gone to a pair who played No. 2 on its own team. They were seeded No. 7, behind teammates John Benson and Tony Giammalva (son of former U.S. Davis Cup star Sammy Giammalva). In the semis, they blasted Stanford's Peter Rennert and Lloyd Bourne, 6-1, 6-0, who had upset the No. 1 seeds, Buehning and Blaine Willenborg of UCLA, 6-2, 6-4. In the finals, they defeated the No. 4 seeds, Andy Kohlberg and Michael Fancutt of Tennessee, 6-2, 7-5, 6-2.

The brilliant coach Glenn Bassett of UCLA did a masterful job in piloting his young Bruins to the team title in '79. They beat a star-studded Trinity team (one of the best never to win the NCAAs) in the finals, 5-3. En route to the title match, they defeated Brigham Young, 5-1, Pepperdine, 5-4, and Stanford, 6-2. Their toughest match actually was against Allen Fox's Pepperdine team, which won the singles, 4-2, but got swept in the doubles.

One of my very best Georgia teams almost beat Pepperdine the day before in the first round, losing a heartbreaker, 5-4.

PETER RENNERT
LEADS STANFORD IN 1980

Bearded Peter Rennert, who grew up on the tennis courts at Port Washington (N.Y.) Academy with another sizzling southpaw, John McEnroe, and who entered Stanford with John as a freshman in 1978, led The Cardinal to the 1980 NCAA team title.

Rennert, who had played No. 4 as a freshman on Stanford's 1978 championship team, was at the No. 1 spot this time, and he won all four of his singles matches and all of his No. 1 doubles matches (with partner Lloyd Bourne).

Coach Dick Gould's men defeated Utah, 6-0; Clemson, 7-2; Pepperdine, 6-3, and their "neighbors" from California-Berkeley in the finals, 5-3, in a very close match. The Bears actually won three of the first four singles to lead 3-1 (only Rennert winning over Scott McCain, 6-2, 6-4), but Scott Bondurant and Jim Gurfein triumphed at No. 4 and No. 6 to tie the score at 3-3 going into the doubles, where Stanford won at both No. 1 and No. 2. Rennert and Bourne clinched the match by upsetting Chris Dunk and Marty Davis, 6-2, 1-6, 6-1, a pair that had won three previous meetings during the '80 season.

It was a heartbreaking loss for Coach Bill Wright's Bears, who had defeated the same Stanford team four months earlier in the finals of the Collegiate Indoor team tournament at Princeton, 5-4, with Davis and Dunk beating Rennert and Bourne, 4-6, 6-4, 6-1, to clinch the match.

Rennert was top seeded in the singles and was impressive in reaching the finals, being extended only by South African Eddie Edwards in the quarters. But he was upset in the finals by the No. 5 seed — the tall, handsome blond Robert Van't Hof of Southern California, 6-4, 6-4. Van't Hof won the semifinals over Princeton's Leif Shiras, 6-1, 6-2. Shiras had upset the No. 2 seed in the second round: Scott McCain of Cal-Berkeley, 6-2, 6-3.

Tennessee's talented Mel Purcell and Rodney Harmon, the No. 1 seeds, came through to win the doubles and keep the California schools from taking home all the silverware. They nipped Rennert and Bourne of Stanford in the semis, 6-4, 7-6, and the No. 2 seeds, John Benson and Tony Giammalva of Trinity in the finals, 7-6 (5-3), 7-6 (5-4).

The year 1980 marked the beginning of two-out-of-three

set finals in NCAA play. From the very beginning, intercollegiate championship finals were the best of five sets, carrying on the tradition originating at the first Wimbledon in 1877, the first U.S. Championships four years later in 1881 and the first U.S. "intercollegiates" in 1883. In those early, formative years of tennis the play was held on grass courts, where points are considerably shorter than on other surfaces, and the matches, therefore, are much less strenuous. But the college coaches finally hauled off and decided to discontinue the long best-of-five-set finals, which frequently lasted longer

Stanford's Peter Rennert congratulates 1980 singles winner Robert Van't Hof of Southern Cal.

than the 26-mile marathon run. They decreed that all matches in the future would be the best of three sets.

I am in favor of the best-of-three-set format for tournaments such as the NCAAs because the players first take part in the grueling team tournament, then play both the singles and doubles tournaments in a short time span that often requires them to play two or three matches per day. But I like the best-of-

Tennessee's Mel Purcell (l) and Rodney Harmon celebrate their doubles crown in 1980.

five-set format for Davis Cup and Grand Slam tournaments when the players get more rest between their matches.

Another first: Georgia's Lindsey Hopkins Indoor Courts fortunately were completed in time for NCAA use because there was an abnormal amount of rainfall. In fact, all eight first-round matches of the team tournament were played indoors, which permitted the championships to stay on schedule.

STANFORD REPEATS IN 1981

Handsome Tim Mayotte stole the show in the 1981 NCAAs in Athens. First, he helped Stanford repeat as NCAA team tournament champion: The Cardinal's fourth triumph in five years and sixth in nine. Second, he won the singles crown, losing only one set in the process; and third, he won collegiate tennis's highly coveted Rafael Osuna Award, which goes to the player best exemplifying sportsmanship, character, academic and competitive excellence. None other than Georgia's Dean Rusk, former United States secretary of state and a Rhodes Scholar, made the presentation.

After playing No. 3 as a freshman and No. 2 as a sophomore (losing in the second round of the NCAAs each year), Mayotte came into his own as a junior in '81. Seeded No. 4, he defeated Drew Gitlin of SMU in the semifinals, 6-2, 6-4. Gitlin had won by default from the No. 1 seed Chip Hooper of Arkansas in the quarterfinals when Hooper had to retire because of leg cramps while holding a slight lead in the third set.

In the finals, Mayotte trimmed his teammate Jim Gurfein, 6-7, 6-3, 6-3. Gurfein played No. 3 for The Cardinal behind Mayotte and Scott Davis, and it was the third time in seven years that players from the same school had met in the finals.

Stanford's Tim Mayotte accepts congratulations from University of Georgia law professor (and former Secretary of State) Dean Rusk.

Stanford's John Whitlinger and Chico Hagey did it in 1974, preceded by Trinity's Dick Stockton and Brian Gottfried in 1972. It has been done only one time since then: Georgia's Mikael Pernfors and George Bezecny squared off in 1985.

Mayotte also became the fifth Stanford player to win the singles since 1973, following in the footsteps of Sandy Mayer, 1973; John Whitlinger, 1974; Matt Mitchell, 1977, and John McEnroe, 1978.

Mayotte a few days later turned professional, forfeiting his final year of collegiate eligibility, as had the three previous

NCAA champions: Robert Van't Hof of USC, 1980; Kevin Curren of Texas, 1979; and John McEnroe of Stanford, 1978.

In the doubles finals, hard-serving David Pate and Karl Richter of TCU, coached by 1948 NCAA doubles champion and great American Davis Cupper Tut Bartzen, upset Arkansas' Australian tandem of Peter Doohan and Pat Serret, 6-7, 6-3, 6-4. The Aussies had twice beaten Pate and Richter during the season, and they were to come back and win the NCAA doubles in 1982.

Pate and Richter were fortunate to get by Georgia's giant lefthanders Bill Rogers (six-three) and John Mangan (six-five) in the semifinals, winning a hard-fought three-setter, 7-6 (5-3), 4-6, 6-3.

Stanford won the team tournament, clinching every match in the singles play. However, Coach Dick Gould did have his men play doubles in two matches because they had not played much doubles during the season (since they won most of the time in the singles) and they needed the practice.

The Cardinal blanked Utah, 9-0; defeated Cal-Berkeley, 5-4, clinching in the singles and defaulting all three doubles; defeated Georgia, 7-2, winning the singles, 5-1, and the doubles, 2-1, in a match much closer than the 7-2 score might indicate. Stanford won three of the singles encounters in three sets, and also won a doubles match in three sets.

In the finals Stanford conquered UCLA, 5-1, in the singles and defaulted all three doubles, but the singles were hard fought: four of The Cardinal's wins coming in three sets. At No. 1, Mayotte nipped Marcel Freeman, 6-7, 7-6, 6-3 in a torrid battle.

Host team Georgia made its best showing ever in the NCAA team tournament, giving champion Stanford a hard match in the semifinals and beating powerful Southern Cal, 6-3, in the third-place playoff. It was the first time Georgia's schedule had permitted a week's rest before the NCAAs. In every previous year Georgia had finished its exhausting SEC tournament just a day before the NCAA team tournament began and, consequently, was too tired to play its best. Finally, the SEC changed its dates so that its players would have a week's rest before the NCAAs — and it paid off for the Bulldogs.

A deep team with eight fine players —Bill Rogers, Brent Crymes, John Mangan, Paul Groth, Tom Foster, Kelly Thurman, Peter Lloyd and Gerald Kleis — this Georgia team was good enough to have won some of the NCAA team tournaments.

AN UNSEEDED SOUTHPAW
TAKES THE 1982 TITLE

Although unseeded, Michigan's 1982 NCAA singles champion Mike Leach was not exactly a stranger at Georgia's Henry Feild Stadium, and he put to good use the experience of three previous NCAA tournaments in Athens — not to mention a powerful serve-and-volley attack that enabled him to nip Pepperdine's battling Brad Gilbert in the finals, 7-5, 6-3.

Leach, who had lost to Georgia's big John Mangan in the team tournament, was lucky to reach the finals. In the semis he was down 5-3 in the third set against the talented South African Christo Steyn of Miami who worked up a 3-0 lead on his own serve: *quadruple match point!* But Leach won four straight points and went on to take a hard-fought tie-breaker and the match, 6-2, 4-6, 7-6 (7-4).

Gilbert, the 1979 national junior college champion, also had a titanic struggle in the semis, finally overcoming the No. 2 seed Marcel Freeman of UCLA, 7-6 (7-3), 7-6 (8-6).

In earlier rounds Leach upset No. 6 seed Pepperdine's Glenn Michibata (the Canadian who played No. 1 for The

Michigan's Mike Leach takes the singles title in 1982.

Wave ahead of Gilbert), and Gilbert toppled No. 4 seed Scott Davis of Stanford.

The No. 1 seed, Rodney Harmon of SMU (who had transferred from Tennessee), was knocked off in the first round by Danny Saltz of UCLA, and Saltz promptly lost the next round to Howard Sands of Harvard, who bowed to Leach.

Leach, who credited his coach Brian Eisner for getting him into excellent physical shape for the grueling NCAAs, became the third lefthander in 11 years to win the title, following in the footsteps of Jimmy Connors of UCLA (1971) and John McEnroe of Stanford (1978).

Leach was Michigan's second NCAA singles champion; big Barry MacKay won it for the Wolverines in 1957. Coincidentally, Leach became the second straight native of Massachusetts to win the NCAA singles. His home in Weston, Mass., is not far from Springfield, home of 1981 champion Tim Mayotte of Stanford.

Arkansas' talented tandem of Peter Doohan and Pat Serrett, the Australians who had lost in the 1981 finals to TCU's David Pate and Karl Richter in an upset, blazed through a tough doubles field this time. They trimmed Georgia's brilliant Allen Miller and Ola Malmqvist in the finals, 7-6 (7-5), 5-7, 6-2.

The team tournament was fiercely contested and had several teams good enough to win it, but the No. 1 seeds, the UCLA Bruins, won the title for the sixth time under master coach Glenn Bassett. They breezed by Harvard in the first round, winning the singles, 5-1, and defaulting all three doubles; then they blanked tough TCU 6-0 in the quarters after the Horned Frogs had upset No. 4 seed Southern Cal in the first round.

UCLA's toughest match came in the semis against a powerful Georgia team that had beaten Michigan, 6-0, and Trinity, 5-2. UCLA won the singles, 4-2, but Georgia's very strong doubles teams almost swept the doubles. Miller and Malmqvist beat Marcel Freeman and Robbie Venter at No. 1, and John Mangan and Peter Lloyd downed John Davis and Blaine Willenborg at No. 2 to tie the score at 4-4. Then UCLA's Danny Saltz and Bobby Berger won a sizzling three-setter from Tom Foster and Deane Frey at No. 3 doubles, 6-2, 4-6, 6-3.

In the finals Pepperdine almost gave Coach Allen Fox a victory over his alma mater (UCLA). At one time Pepperdine was winning five of the six singles, but the Bruins rallied to win everything but No. 1, Michibata beating Marcel Freeman, 6-3, 6-3. Freeman, however, wound up as the nation's No. 1 player in the final rankings. He and SMU's Rodney Harmon had the two best records in the country entering the NCAA championships, but Harmon lost in the first round while Freeman went all the way to the semis.

THE M & M BOYS BECOME GEORGIA'S FIRST NCAA CHAMPIONS IN 1983

Georgia's elongated doubles duo of Allen Miller (six-three) and Ola Malmqvist from Sweden (six-seven) became the school's first NCAA champions by winning the individual doubles title. Although they had captured the tough ITCA National Indoors the previous year, injuries to both of them during the '83 season prevented them from compiling a record good enough even to get seeded in the NCAAs. But they finally were healthy in May, and they won six straight matches en route to a great victory in the finals over the No. 2 seeds, Ken Flach and Robert Seguso of Southern Illinois-Edwardsville, 7-5, 6-3. (Flach and Seguso went on to win both Wimbledon and the U.S. Open diadems.) Miller and Malmqvist toppled No. 1 seeded Roberto Saad (Argentina) and Paul Smith (New Zealand) of Wichita State in the semis, 7-5, 4-6, 6-3.

Allen was only a sophomore when he teamed with Ola, "the genial giant," for the championship. The year before, when both were new to the team (Ola having transferred from Central Florida), they wasted no time establishing themselves as one of the best college doubles teams in the nation — despite starting the year as Georgia's No. 3 team. After winning their division at the Clemson Classic — the first tournament of the fall — the M & M boys brought home the gold from the tough Southern Collegiates, beating the top three seeds in succession.

Winning the title in that formidable field of 64 teams earned the brash rookies a trip to the ITA National Indoors at Princeton in January 1982, and guess who won there? The M & M Boys upset four veteran teams in a row: Pate and Richter of TCU, the 1981 NCAA champions, in the first round; Flach and Seguso of SIU-Edwardsville; Venter and Freeman of UCLA; and Gallien and Van Nostrand of Pepperdine in the finals, 6-3, 3-6, 6-3.

Ola Malmqvist (l) and Allen Miller (r) become Georgia's first NCAA champions in 1983.

By now I was thinking that Allen and Ola were good enough to win Georgia's first NCAA tennis title, which they damned near did in May when they barely lost in the finals. Allen and Ola came back in '83 determined to win this coveted crown, but both suffered injuries in February that kept them below par throughout the winter and spring. Only when The Big One rolled around in May were the M & M boys in top form, and now nothing could stop them. Their brilliant win over Flach and Seguso in the finals constituted Georgia's greatest accomplishment in tennis at that time!

Miller, by the way, was an absolute wizard in doubles, with the best instinct for poaching I have ever seen. He had no weaknesses and could do it all. His serve was not powerful, but it was one of those deceptive lefthanded types, and he could slice or spin it. Ola utilized his tremendous height and had the most powerful cannonball serve in the college ranks. The two were tough to break. Furthermore, they had impenetrable command of the net where they were outstanding volleyers and strong on the overhead. Allen received serve in the backhand court and was the most reliable I have seen in getting the return safely back in play.

Allen went on to team with the great Mikael Pernfors for the next two years. They never won the NCAAs, but reached the semis both years, and they did rank No. 1 in the final 1985 national rankings. They had the best overall season record and had beaten the NCAA champs from Pepperdine twice during the season (Kelly Jones and Carlos DiLaura).

In fact, Miller owns the best-average finish in NCAA play in modern times: finalist and winner with Malmqvist, twice a semifinalist with Pernfors. Counting team tournament doubles matches, Miller's four-year NCAA doubles record was 22-4; Pepperdine's Kelly Jones has the second-best mark at 21-5, followed by Rick Leach of USC at 19-3.

But back to the '83 tournament, Utah's hustling Greg Holmes became the first two-handed hitter off both sides to win the NCAA singles and also the first player from the Western Athletic Conference to do so.

In a fast field that saw only three of the seeds reach the quarterfinals (No. 1 Holmes, No. 3 Rodney Harmon of SMU and No. 4 Johnny Levine of Texas), Holmes was invincible in marching over six foes, losing only one set — in the semifinals against hard-serving David Pate of TCU, who had upset No. 7 Eric Korita of SMU and No. 4 Levine on the way.

The Holmes-Pate match was a classic, Holmes taking the long three-setter 7-5, 4-6, 7-6. The third set tie-breaker went to 11-9.

In the finals Holmes made short work of Minnesota's unseeded Fredrik Pahlett of Sweden, 6-2, 6-2. Pahlett had upset No. 8 seed Miami's Christo Steyn of South Africa in a second-round squeaker, 5-7, 6-1, 7-6 (7-1) and No. 3 seed Harmon in the semis, 4-6, 6-4, 7-5. Pahlett later that year in November was to win the Volvo All-America in Los Angeles.

A native of Danville, Ca., Holmes first came into collegiate prominence by reaching the finals of the Prince-Nike ITCA National Indoors at Princeton in February earlier in 1983. He lost to Princeton's Ted Farnsworth, 6-4, 6-3, after barely getting by Georgia's Allen Miller in the quarters, 6-2, 2-6, 7-5.

All the coaches were especially pleased that a protégé of Utah's veteran and popular coach Harry James (later to be enshrined into the Collegiate Hall of Fame) captured the coveted NCAA crown. Harry, who died several years later, coached the Utes 26 years from a wheelchair because of leg injuries sustained in World War II, and he made Utah a national power.

Another strong field was on hand for the 1983 team tournament, and for the first time in history there was not a single upset among the seeded teams until the finals, when Dennis Ralston's splendid SMU Mustangs, seeded No. 1, fell to Dick Gould's equally superb Stanford crew, seeded No. 2, by 5-4.

Stanford had barely made the final round, winning a hard-fought semifinal match over Southern California, seeded No. 3, by another 5-4 count, the clinching point being scored at No. 2 doubles by Mark McKeen and Jim Grabb over Matt Anger and Anthony Emerson (son of the great Australian world champion Roy Emerson) in three sensational tie-break

Utah's Greg Holmes takes the singles crown.

sets: 6-7 (1-7), 7-6 (7-2) and 7-6 (7-5)!

The Stanford-SMU finals was another thriller. Scott Davis, John Letts, Eric Rosenfeld and Jim Grabb gave Stanford a 4-2 lead in the singles, but the Mustangs tied the count at 4-4 with victories at No. 2 doubles by Rodney Harmon and Eric Van't Hof and at No. 3 by John Ross and Kim Forsythe. The team match hinged on the No. 1 doubles, which saw The Cardinal's Davis and Letts win over Jerome Vanier (France) and Eric Korita, 7-6 (7-5), 6-4.

Thus Stanford became champion for the fifth time in seven years.

The year 1983 also marked the origin of the Collegiate Tennis Hall of Fame. Although the Hall of Fame building was not built until 1984, fifteen of collegiate tennis's all-time great players and coaches were inducted in ceremonies Wednesday afternoon, May 18 (the "rest" day between the NCAA team tournament and individual championships).

Kenny Rogers and SMU coach Dennis Ralston (former Wimbledon doubles champion) won the Celebrity Doubles event, which attracted such stars as Lyle Waggoner (the handsome "hunk" of Carol Burnett's TV show), Christopher Atkins (co-star with Brooke Shields in *The Blue Lagoon*) and Pat Harrington, Jr. (better known as Schneider, the macho apartment super of "One Day at a Time").

It was another major step in the growth of the NCAAs in Athens.

BASSETT VERSUS GOULD, AGAIN, IN 1984

In 1984 master coaches Glenn Bassett of UCLA and Dick Gould of Stanford steered their respective alma maters to the finals of the NCAA team tournament for the fifth time in the eight-year history of the event.

It was the third time they had squared off against each other in the finals at Henry Feild Stadium, and this time Bassett's Bruins emerged victorious, 5-4, in a six-hour marathon that avenged UCLA losses to Stanford in the 1978 and 1981 finals.

It also was the fourth time UCLA and Stanford had met during the 1984 season, UCLA having won two of the three previous bouts.

The singles were split. Jeff Klaparda at No. 2, Mark Basham at No. 4 and Craig Venter at No. 6 won for UCLA; Dan Goldie at No. 1, Jim Grabb at No. 3 and Derrick Rostagno at No. 5 countered for Stanford. In the doubles, Rostagno-McKeen put Stanford ahead by winning No. 3 over Jim Pugh and David Livingston, but Klaparda and Venter won for UCLA at No. 2 over Goldie-Rosenfeld to knot the team score at 4-4. In a thrilling three-setter Michael Kures and Basham won at No. 1 over Letts and Grabb, 6-1, 3-6, 6-4, to give UCLA its 15th NCAA team title.

UCLA's victory also marked the 12th straight year that a Pac-10 school had won the team crown (Trinity was the last non-California school to win it, back in 1972, also in Athens).

The semifinal matches were hotly contested, too. UCLA edged Pepperdine, 5-3, after splitting the singles; Stanford beat Georgia, 5-3, also splitting the singles.

In the tournament's biggest upset, No. 8 seed Georgia knocked off No. 2 seed Southern Cal, 5-4, in the quarters in a sensational match that was forced indoors by rain for the conclusion of the No. 1 doubles battle. Two of the NCAA's best tandems of modern history were squared off: Georgia's Allen Miller and Mikael Pernfors and USC's Rick Leach and Tim Pawsat. Miller and Pernfors prevailed, 7-6 (7-3), 4-6, 6-2.

Georgia had won the singles, 4-2, getting wins from Pernfors at No. 1, Miller at No. 3, George Bezecny at No. 4

Mikael Pernfors acknowledging his 1984 singles crown, with Tut Bartzen, chairman of the NCAA Tennis Committee.

and Jeff Wallace at No. 6. But Coach Dick Leach's powerful doubles lineup quickly squared the match by winning both No. 2 doubles (Jorge Lozano and Todd Witsken) and No. 3 (Matt Anger and Anthony Emerson).

In the ensuing singles tournament, Georgia's little Swede Mikael Pernfors (at only five-seven) continued his winning ways. He had won all four of his singles matches at No. 1 in the team tournament and was seeded No. 4 in the singles event behind Tennessee's Paul Annacone (who had nipped

Former Wimbledon and NCAA champions Dennis Ralston (USC) and Arthur Ashe (UCLA) at Hall of Fame ceremonies in '84.

Pernfors a week earlier in the finals of the SEC singles), Texas's Johnny Levine and Clemson's Lawson Duncan.

Auburn's unseeded Barry Moir, of South Africa, knocked off his fellow SEC star, No. 1 Annacone, in the quarters, 7-6 (7-5), 6-4, but fell in the semis to Duncan of Clemson, 6-0, 6-4.

In the other semifinal, Pernfors rallied to upset No. 2 Levine, 1-6, 7-6 (7-2), 6-2.

In the finals, it was a classic backcourt battle between two of the best forehands in NCAA history, Pernfors prevailing, 6-1, 6-4.

"I thought I was too tired [from the many matches he had played] to play my best," commented Pernfors afterwards. "But the Parris Island Marine Band [which played a concert of martial music just prior to the finals] fired me up, and really helped me get off to a good start."

The Jones Boys of Pepperdine (no relation), Kelly and Jerome, maintained their No. 1 seeding and captured the doubles crown, defeating Rick Leach and Tim Pawsat, who avenged a loss to Miller and Pernfors of Georgia in the team tournament by beating the Bulldogs in the semis, 6-2, 6-2.

In the Hall of Fame ceremonies, the new building donated by Kenny and Marianne Rogers was officially dedicated. Kenny and Dennis Ralston repeated as Celebrity Doubles champions, edging former Wimbledon doubles champion Gardnar Mulloy of Miami and the Atlanta Braves' home-run king Hank Aaron in the finals.

GEORGIA FINALLY KEEPS
THE TROPHY AT HOME IN 1985

Georgia won the 1985 NCAA team tournament for several reasons: first, it had one of the most powerful singles lineups in NCAA annals; second, it had the No. 1 doubles team in the country; and third, it was, in my opinion, Mikael Pernfors' resolve to lead his team to the coveted team title.

I was disappointed that our 1984 team had not won it all. It was the same lineup as that in 1985 except senior Jeff Wallace had graduated and had been replaced by another strong No. 6 man: freshman Trey Carter. In 1984 we were seeded only No. 8, but we played a great match in the quarters to upset the No. 2 seed, one of Dick Leach's finest USC teams, 5-4. Frankly, we were just too tired to play our best in the semis the next morning against No. 3 Stanford. Although we split the singles, Stanford proved too strong in the doubles.

But I was confident we had a very good chance to "take the cake" in '85.

As anyone knows, a coach must not only assemble talent good enough to win but also must avoid tough luck (like injuries, illness, etc.); and he must get his share of good breaks. In 1985, everything went in our favor, including the important fact that our team was well rested for every match.

After cruising by Harvard, 6-2, in the first round, we did have a hard match with No. 3 Stanford in the quarters; but none of the matches went three sets (we won 5-3). So we were relatively fresh for the big semifinal bout against No. 2 seed Southern California.

Pernfors at No. 1, Deane Frey at No. 4, soph Philip Johnson at No. 5 and freshman Trey Carter at No. 6 all scored straight-set wins as we took the singles, 4-2, from the favored Trojans. But I was very much worried about Bezecny, who had become dehydrated after losing a long three-setter to Jorge Lozano at No. 2. George had to go to the hospital for treatment, but he snapped back and was ready to play the next day.

Our team was sky high emotionally for the finals, playing before a monster overflow crowd of 5,000-plus. We jumped to a 2-1 lead with Pernfors winning at No. 1 over Michael Kures, 6-2, 6-3; Miller at No. 3 over Brad Pearce, 6-4, 6-4, and Frey losing at No. 4 to Mark Basham, 6-1, 7-5. Then Carter put us ahead by winning at No. 6 over Ken Diller, 7-6 (7-0), 3-6, 6-3, to make the team score 3-1.

At this point, both the No. 2 singles (Bezecny vs. Jeff Klaparda) and No. 5 (Johnson vs. Brett Greenwood) were in the third sets in toss-up battles. I was "working" Bezecny's match on the upper courts while assistant coach Manuel Diaz was with Johnson on the bottom battery. All of a sudden Mikael Pernfors yelled to me that Johnson had triple match point, but I didn't hear any more cheers and figured he must have lost them. In the meantime Bezecny came through, winning 2-6, 6-4, 6-3 to give us a commanding 4-1 lead. I immediately tried to get to the bottom courts, but the

Coach Magill aloft after clinching the 1985 team championship.

area was so crowded with almost hysterical fans that I couldn't make my way through them. So I jumped up on top of the umpire's stand on court No. 3 in order to see the action on court No. 5.

Johnson, indeed, had blown several match points, the score was tied 5-5 in the third set, and Philip seemed downhearted.

I hollered to him at the top of my voice, "FIGHT IT OUT, PHILIP! FIGHT IT OUT!"

The Dalton Detonator did "fight it out." He reached another match point at 6-5, worked his way to the net and walloped a two-handed crosscourt volley for the title-winning point, causing pandemonium to break out amongst the delirious Georgia fans. They hoisted Philip on their shoulders, and, a few minutes later, they even toted me from the bottom courts up to the main grandstand in what was the happiest moment of my many hours devoted to building up University of Georgia tennis.

A gracious Glenn Bassett, UCLA's famed coach, said to the huge partisan crowd at the awards ceremonies:

"If any team ever deserved this championship it was your Georgia Bulldogs this week. They made history by defeating the top three seeded teams on successive days. Congratulations!"

In Mikael Pernfors' "swan song" in the NCAAs, he repeated his incredible performance of the previous year: unbeaten in both the team tournament and individual singles (10-0). In the team play he defeated Larry Scott of Harvard; Dan Goldie of Stanford (the 6-1, 6-1 score thoroughly avenging his loss to Goldie in the National Indoor finals); Todd Witsken of USC; and Michael Kures of UCLA.

Although exhausted mentally and physically from leading Georgia to the team title, Mikael the very next day began his drive to repeat as singles champion. He won six in a row to do it: Merzbacher of Minnesota, DiLaura of Pepperdine,

DeVries of California-Berkeley, Connell of Texas A&M, Grabb of Stanford, and Bezecny of Georgia.

Henry Feild Stadium had another 4,000-plus full house for the Pernfors-Bezecny finals, which also was the last match in which the great American umpire Mike Blanchard sat in the chair. Despite the huge throng on hand, the match also was notable for the least crowd excitement in the history of a big tennis match. The all-Georgia crowd was too polite to cheer much for either player, since it didn't want to show favoritism. Pernfors was at his best, closing out his magnificent Bulldog career with a 6-2, 6-3 triumph and thus becoming the first and last player to win this rugged tournament in consecutive years since Southern Cal's great Dennis Ralston in 1963–64.

The center court on which Pernfors won his brace of NCAA crowns now is named for this little Swede who possessed all the necessary ingredients to be a great champion: a repertoire of super shots, tremendous athletic agility and quickness, the will to win and the heart of a lion. He also played with gusto and was a wonderful sportsman, too. I have never known a more respected and popular player amongst his peers than Mikael Bengt Pernfors of Hollviksnas, Sweden.

By the way, Georgia almost performed the "hat trick" by winning the doubles title as well. Miller and Pernfors were top-seeded but fell in the semifinals to a team they had twice defeated during the season: Pepperdine's Kelly Jones and Carlos DiLaura (a Chilean Davis Cupper). However, Pernfors and Miller did receive the final No. 1 ranking by ITA, based on their superior season record. Jones and DiLaura went on to win the finals over Royce Deppe and Charles Beckmann of Texas, 7-5, 7-6 (8-6). It was the second straight doubles title for Kelly Jones who had won the previous year with Jerome Jones (no relation).

THE PAC-10 RETURNS
TO PROMINENCE IN 1986

After yielding most of the honors to a non-California school for the first time in 13 years, the PAC-10 powers returned with a vengeance in 1986 to sweep everything in sight.

Although seeded only No. 6 (like Georgia in 1985) Stanford stormed to its eighth NCAA team title for Coach Dick Gould — their sixth victory in Athens. The Cardinal players defeated intrastate rival Pepperdine in the finals, 5-2. They won the singles, 4-2, with a powerful 1-2-3 lineup of Dan Goldie, Jim Grabb and Patrick McEnroe. The clinching point was scored by McEnroe (younger brother of the redoubtable John) and John Letts at No. 2 doubles over Robbie Weiss and Gilberto Cicero, 6-2, 6-3.

In the semis, Stanford toppled No. 2 seed UCLA, 5-1, and Pepperdine, seeded No. 5, upset the No. 1 team, Southern Methodist, 5-1, in a shocker. Champion Stanford's toughest match actually came in the quarterfinals against No. 3 Clemson, The Cardinal prevailing, 5-3. Clemson's Jay Berger upset Dan Goldie (later to win the singles tournament), and the Tigers' No. 2 player Richard Matuszewski toppled highly-regarded Jim Grabb. Clemson wound up splitting the six singles matches. But Stanford rallied to win both No. 1 doubles (Goldie-Grabb over Matuszewski-Brandon Walters) and No. 2 (McEnroe-Letts over Brian Page-Matt Frooman).

After leading Stanford to the team title, Dan Goldie (like Pernfors the previous year) captured the coveted singles crown. Seeded No. 3, Goldie defeated SMU's ace, Richey Reneberg, seeded No. 8, in the finals, 6-2, 6-1.

Georgia's Trey Carter, a freshman on Georgia's championship team in 1985, almost scored a super first round upset over No. 4 seed Kelly Jones of Pepperdine, but finally lost, 7-6 (8-6), 5-7, 6-3.

Celebrity Doubles in 1986: (l-r) Cox Enterprises CEO Jim Kennedy, Wimbledon champion Dick Savitt, Pepperdine coach Allen Fox, and USTA president David Markin.

One of the standouts of the tournament was Furman's three-sport star Ned Caswell of Atlanta, who had often played on the same courts as a boy in the Crackerland juniors. He knocked off Stanford's Patrick McEnroe in the first round, and then played a great match with No. 4 Kelly Jones of Pepperdine, finally yielding, 3-6, 6-3, 7-6 (10-8).

Caswell, at a track meet for Furman a few days before the tournament began, had won the 100-yard dash in the fantastic time of 9.3 seconds!

Kelly Jones failed in his noble bid to win the doubles title three straight years with a different partner. He and his third partner, Augustine Moreno, fell victim to UCLA's Michael Kures and big Dan Nahirny in the quarters, 6-3, 7-5.

The No. 1 seeds, Rick Leach and Tim Pawsat of USC, defeated Kures and Nahirny in the finals, 6-7 (3-7), 6-4, 6-2.

ANOTHER LAUREL
FOR THE BULLDOGS IN 1987

When our veteran Georgia team of 1985 won the NCAAs, I was not surprised because we had pretty much the same outfit that had almost won it the previous year. But I was pleasantly surprised two years later when our 1987 team, including two freshmen and three sophomores, came on like gangbusters at the end of the season and proved to be a worthy although unexpected winner.

After losing Pernfors, Bezecny, Miller and Frey by graduation in 1985, we began a rebuilding program the next year, bringing in three promising freshmen: Stephen Enochs of Greensboro, N.C.; T. J. Middleton of Dallas, Texas; and Gerald Thonhauser of Vienna, Austria, recommended by former Georgia All-American and assistant coach Norman Holmes, who was married to an Austrian and taught tennis in Graz, Austria. Unfortunately, the talented Thonhauser didn't like to attend classes and flunked out of school after one year.

However, we had plenty of material when we began "boot camp" in early September 1986: one senior, captain Philip Johnson, a star on the 1985 NCAA champions and the best player in the rugged Southeastern conference; also two other members of the 1985 national champions, junior Trey Carter and junior Phillip Roberts (a hard-serving doubles specialist).

Our other scholarshipped players were sophomores Enochs and Middleton, who had enjoyed impressive freshman seasons, and sophomore John Boytim, a transfer from Texas and a former U.S. junior champion. Finally, we had two promising freshmen recruits: Mike Morrison, four-time Illinois high school champion, and Jim Childs of Atlanta, 1985 U.S. Interscholastic doubles champion with Enochs and singles finalist to Al Parker.

Two more good boys, both walk-ons, rounded out this very strong squad: junior Tim Ruotolo, a transfer from

William & Mary, and sophomore Billy Chocallo, former No. 1 junior in Georgia.

This group made outstanding showings in fall, winter and spring play, improving all the time. Look at what they did in the fall quarter of 1986: Clemson Classic — Johnson won the A-flight singles; Southern Collegiates — Boytim defeated Enochs in an all-Georgia singles finals; Georgia Tech Classic — Enochs defeated Childs in all-Georgia singles finals, and Roberts-Chocallo defeated Enochs-Middleton in all-Georgia doubles finals; ITCA Region Three Indoors — Johnson defeated Johan Donar of Miami in the singles finals; Volvo All-America in Los Angeles — Johnson defeated Shelby Cannon of Tennessee in the quarters and lost in the semis to the nation's No. 1 player, Richey Reneberg of SMU.

The team began the winter quarter by winning a thrilling SEC Indoor tournament in Athens, nipping Tennessee 15 to 14. In the ITCA-USTA National Indoor team tournament at Louisville, Georgia defeated Minnesota, 5-1, and LSU, 5-4, to gain the semifinals. But the marathon match against LSU ended at two o'clock in the morning, and we had to play a rested up and strong Clemson team early the next afternoon. The Tigers whipped us, 5-2, and then lost to USC in the finals.

In spring dual matches Georgia compiled a fine 18-2 record, winning the toughest conference in the land with a perfect 9-0 round-robin record and also taking the toughest region (Region Three) with a perfect 15-0 record. Our only disappointments were a tough loss to No. 1 seed Southern Cal in the Blue-Gray tournament in Montgomery, and another loss to Clemson — this time on their courts. We hoped for a chance at revenge.

When the draw was announced for the NCAA team tournament, our team was pleased to be the No. 4 seed, behind Southern California, Cal-State Long Beach and SMU. We were especially jubilant about drawing Clemson in the first match, and we were really up for it.

We exacted the revenge we were looking for, winning handily, 5-2. We took four of the six singles and clinched it at No. 3 doubles with our outstanding No. 3 tandem of Johnson and Childs.

In the quarters, we played No. 5 seed Pepperdine, an old rival in the NCAA tournament. We won the singles, 4-2, with Johnson scoring an upset over the No. 2 ranked player in the country, Canadian Andre Sznaidjer, 3-6, 6-4, 6-1, at No. 1 singles; Stephen Enochs also upset Robbie Weiss at No. 2 singles, 6-3, 7-6 (8-6). (A year later Weiss won the NCAA singles.) Once again our splendid No. 3 doubles duo of Johnson and Childs clinched the match.

We were confident we could beat Southern Cal in the semis the next day, even though they were heavy favorites — undefeated, ranked No. 1 in the country, and riding a red-hot 32-match winning streak. LSU had given us some extra encouragement by extending the Trojans in the quarters. Coach Jerry Simmons' Bayou Bengals split the singles with the Trojans, but Coach Dick Leach's always powerful doubles teams clinched the match by taking both No. 1 and No. 2.

I had hoped we would win at least four of the six singles matches from USC in the semis, but we split. Leach was red hot in beating Johnson at No. 1, 6-3, 6-1. Carter at No. 3 and Middleton at No. 6 lost three-setters to Scott Melville and Eric Amend, respectively, but Enochs upset Luke Jensen in three sets at No. 2, and Boytim and Morrison both came through at No. 3 and No. 5.

I'm sure Coach Leach (Rick's father) thought he'd handle us in the doubles, but I had supreme confidence in our No. 2 and No. 3 teams. Sure enough, the Trojans' great No. 1 team, Leach and Melville (who later won the NCAA tournament) dispatched Enochs and Boytim in straight sets. A few minutes later Johnson and Childs came through for the third

Jim Childs (l) and Philip Johnson celebrate their big win over Southern Cal in the '87 team tournament.

straight day at No. 3 to make the team score, 4-4. And then Carter and Middleton, whom I had dubbed our "swat team" because they were great in the clutch, upset Jensen and Amend, 7-5, 6-3, and we were in the finals once again!

In the finals against Glenn Bassett's always strong UCLA Bruins we were fortunate to win, 5-1, the same score by which we had won in the 1985 finals. But three of our singles victories were hard-fought three-setters (Enochs at No. 2, Boytim at No. 3 and Middleton at No. 6). Furthermore, Johnson at No. 1 was trailing UCLA's ace, big Dan Nahirney, 4-6, 1-2 when Nahirney sustained a badly broken ankle and had to retire.

In the individual tournament, Miami's Andrew Burrow, seeded only No. 7, became the ninth foreigner (and second

South African) to win the singles crown, following in the footsteps of Pennsylvania's Ed Dewhurst of New Zealand, 1903 and 1905; Miami's Francisco Segura of Ecuador, 1943, '44 and '45; Tulane's Jose Aguero of Brazil, 1955; Southern Cal's Alex Olmedo of Peru, 1956 and '58; Southern Cal's Rafael Osuna of Mexico, 1962; Southern Cal's Joaquin Loyo-Mayo of Mexico, 1969; Texas's Kevin Curren of South Africa, 1979; and Georgia's Mikael Pernfors of Sweden, 1984 and '85.

It was unbelievable the way the singles seeds bit the dust, starting in the very first round when No. 2 Andrew Sznaidjer of Pepperdine fell to Paul Mancini of West Virginia; No. 4 Steve DeVries of Cal-Berkely bowed to Tom Mercer of TCU; No. 5 Luke Jensen of USC lost to Den Bishop of SMU; and No. 8 Stefan Kruger of SMU lost to Phil Williamson of Columbia.

Five more seeds tumbled in the second round, including No. 1 Richey Reneberg of SMU (the finalist the previous year) to Shelby Cannon of Tennessee, and No. 3 Philip Johnson of Georgia to Brett Greenwood of UCLA.

No. 6 Rick Leach of USC lost in the round of 16 to Furman's great all-round athlete Ned Caswell, 7-5, 6-7 (4-7), 7-5, following which he also lost his cool. He jumped up on top of a car in the parking lot and started pounding it with his racquet. Eventually he had to be restrained by campus police.

Only two seeds made it to the quarterfinals: No. 7 Burrow of Miami and 9-16 Mark Kaplan of California-Irvine. Burrow won in the quarters over Cannon of Tennessee, and Kaplan defeated unseeded Scott Warner of Nevada-Las Vegas. In the other quarterfinals Oklahoma's Olivier Lorin, a Frenchman, conquered Caswell, and Dan Goldberg of Michigan defeated another non-seed, big Greg Van Emburgh of Kentucky.

In the semifinals, Burrow trimmed Kaplan, 7-6 (7-1), 2-6,

6-1, and Goldberg licked Lorin in another three-setter, 6-4, 2-6, 6-1.

Following the style, the finals naturally went three sets with Burrow winning a backcourt duel, 2-6, 6-1, 6-4, and becoming the first Miami player to win the title since Pancho Sequra's last title in 1945.

Why so many upsets? One main reason: the college field seems to get faster and faster through the years because so many good players are being developed all over the world. In my opinion, the best are not any better than the best of previous eras but there are terrific players not getting by the first round now.

As for the doubles tournament, the NCAA Tennis Committee somehow allowed USC's Rick Leach, despite his earlier temper tantrum, to remain in the tournament (the NCAA head man in Kansas City later reprimanded the committee for not taking severe action). Rick must have had enough time to calm down because he regained his poise and utilized his great talent, along with partner Scott Melville, to capture the doubles for the second time (he won with Tim Pawsat in 1986). Seeded No. 3, they defeated Darren Yates and Julian Barham of Cal-Irvine in the finals, 4-6, 6-4, 7-5.

I should add that I couldn't fully enjoy Georgia's team championship because of the complaints (aired by the media) of coaches Chuck Kriese of Clemson and Dick Leach of USC, who said their teams lost to Georgia because the partisan Bulldog fans gave Georgia too much of a home-court advantage, adding that the tournament therefore should not be continued in Athens.

Of course, the NCAA Tennis Committee considered their complaints "sour grapes," but I let the committee know that the University of Georgia would be happy to bow out: "We don't want to hold the tournament in Athens if the coaches don't want it here," I said. "In fact, I wish you would schedule it some place else, and then if you want it back in Athens we'll put it on again."

The committee replied that we were under contract to hold it again in 1988, that they were not even considering holding it anywhere else in '88, and that they appreciated everything we had done through the years in making it a super event.

So I said, "Well, schedule it somewhere else in 1989."

Southern Cal bid for the 1989 edition to be held at Indian Wells, Ca., at Charley Pasarell's wonderful layout, but just a few months before the 1989 tournament, the NCAA chairman phoned to ask if Georgia could host it again on such short notice. We agreed to put it on, but the 1990 tournament *was* played at Indian Wells and it lost a pot full of money. So the NCAA asked me if Georgia would take it back in 1991.

I said, "We'll be glad to host it, but remember that Georgia never asked for the tournament to be held in Athens in the first place, back in 1972, and we didn't know that we were not supposed to win it."

The truth is, of course, that the University of Georgia and all of us in Athens who put on this great event are proud and honored that the NCAA has awarded the NCAAs to Athens so many times.

CALIFORNIA REDUX IN 1988

California schools made a clean sweep of the titles in the 1988 NCAAs for the fourth time since the team tournament began in 1977.

Dick Gould's favored Stanford men ran roughshod over Texas, 5-0; Kentucky, 5-2; No. 3 seed Southern Cal, 5-3, in the semis; and No. 2 LSU, 5-2, in the finals. Stanford was extended by Dick Leach's Trojans in the semis, splitting the singles but came back strong to win both No. 2 doubles (Patrick McEnroe and Martin Blackman) and No. 3 (Jeff Cathrall and Eric Peus).

McEnroe was the only veteran from Stanford's last NCAA championship team two years earlier (1986). Coach Gould's latest championship outfit was led by freshman David Wheaton, sophomore Jeff Tarango and senior McEnroe.

Coach Jerry Simmons' Bayou Bengal Tigers of LSU fought for their lives to reach the finals. In the quarters they nipped Georgia, 5-3, splitting the singles after Georgia had almost clinched the match in the singles. The next day LSU did the same thing to beat Michigan, 5-4, in the semis: they split the singles, and their No. 1 and No. 3 doubles teams came through again as they did against Georgia.

Perhaps the best match of the tournament came in the round of 16 when Georgia and UCLA battled six hours, with the Bulldogs barely winning, 5-4.

Before the match Coach Glenn Bassett had said to me, "I believe this is a match between the two best teams in the tournament; the winner will win the title." But in beating UCLA we shot our wad and faded in the third sets in both singles and doubles the next day against LSU. Against UCLA our No. 1 and No. 2 doubles teams did a fabulous job in upsetting UCLA's powerful teams that a week later played each other in the doubles tournament finals: No. 1 Pat Galbraith and Brian Garrow, who lost to our Al Parker and Chris Garner 7-5, 5-7, 6-4, and No. 2 Buff Farrow and Robert Bierens who lost to T. J. Middleton and Trey Carter 6-3, 5-7, 6-3.

Pepperdine's backcourt battler Robbie Weiss, coached by former NCAA singles and doubles champion Allen Fox (UCLA), won the singles title over a very tough field, being one of only three seeds (he was top-seeded) to make it to the quarterfinals. He defeated his crosstown rival Brian Garrow of UCLA, unseeded, in a three-set finals, 6-2, 4-6, 6-3.

I had thought Georgia freshman Al Parker would be a strong contender for the title, but he missed three months of the season because of a serious back injury and had not regained top form when he returned to action just a few days before the NCAAs. He had begun his collegiate career in sensational form in the fall by winning the tough Southern Collegiate singles and doubles, and a few weeks later capturing the rugged Region Three Indoor singles. But in late January he sustained the back injury in the quarters of the SEC indoors and was out for three months.

Al, however, made a valiant effort to win the 1988 NCAAs. In the team tournament he lost to Buff Farrow of UCLA and Jeff Brown of LSU, and almost was upset in the individual singles tournament first round by Craig Johnson of Pepperdine, but those matches must have tuned him up because he was brilliant in winning his next three matches: over Canadian Mark Greenan of Wake Forest (who had upset No. 4 Shelby Cannon of Tennessee), Greg Failla of California-Long Beach (seeded 9-16) and Mark Kaplan of Cal-Irvine. But Weiss proved too tough in the semis, winning, 6-3, 6-2.

In the other semifinal, Garrow upset his teammate, No. 5 seed Buff Farrow, 7-6, 6-4.

It was an all-UCLA doubles finals with Pat Galbraith and Garrow defeating Farrow and Bierens, 6-3, 6-2. (Galbraith has gone on to become one of the top professional doubles players in the world.) The No. 1 seeds, Eric Amend and Scott Melville of USC, fell in the semis to Farrow and Bierens, 6-3, 6-4. Melville had won the previous year with Rick Leach, and Amend won the next year with South African Byron Black (now one of the world's top pro doubles players).

DARKHORSE DONNI LEAYCRAFT
TAKES THE '89 CROWN

In the 1989 edition of the NCAAs, Louisiana State's hard-hitting baseliner Donni Leaycraft, from the suburbs of New Orleans (Metairie), became only the fifth singles champion in history who was not the No. 1 player on his team. Leaycraft played No. 2 behind the Tigers' Johan Kjellstien of Sweden who was seeded No. 3 in the NCAAs; Leaycraft was seeded in the second eight.

Other non-No. 1 men to win the NCAAs were Jose Aguero of Tulane, a Brazilian, in 1955 when his teammate Ham Richardson, the defending champion, passed up the NCAAs to perform at Wimbledon; Bob Lutz of Southern Cal in 1967 (the Trojans' No. 1 man and top seed Stan Smith was upset by UCLA's Gary Rose in the quarters); Jimmy Connors of UCLA in 1971, who as a freshman played behind 1970 NCAA champion Jeff Borowiak and Pakistani Davis Cup star Haroon Rahim; and Jared Palmer of Stanford in 1991, who played behind Alex O'Brien (NCAA winner the next year) and Jonathan Stark.

Leaycraft, in fact, had lost to Stanford's No. 2 player Martin Blackman in the team tournament, but he came back to down six good players in winning the singles tournament impressively: Lee Galway of Boise State, Mark Mance of Duke, Conny Falk of Miami, and No. 7 seed Al Parker of Georgia in the quarters; Francisco Montana of Georgia in the semis (Montana had upset No. 1 seed Malivai Washington of Michigan in the first round, 6-4, 6-3); and unseeded Stephen Jung of Nebraska in the finals, 6-1, 4-6, 6-3. (Jung had upset Georgia's Stephen Enochs in the semis, 6-3, 6-2.)

California players, the perennial powers, came back to dominate the doubles, occupying all four semifinal spots. Southern Cal's Byron Black of Zimbabwe, and Eric Amend, although unseeded, knocked off five good teams to win the title. In the semis they beat Mark Kaplan and Richard Lubner of Cal-Irvine; and in the finals they nipped Mike Briggs and Trevor Kronemann of Cal-Irvine, 7-5, 6-7, 7-5.

The defending doubles champions and No. 1 seeds, Pat Galbraith and Brian Garrow of UCLA, were toppled in the second round by fellow Californians Kaplan and Lubner, 6-0, 6-3.

Top-seeded Stanford successfully defended its team title, defeating a strong Georgia team in the finals, 5-3.

Dick Gould's men first disposed of Miami, 5-1, then LSU in the quarters, 5-3, and South Carolina in the semis, 5-2 (the Gamecocks had upset No. 3 Cal-Berkeley in the quarters, 5-4).

Georgia walloped Southern Cal, unseeded for the first time in the team tournament's history, 5-1, in the round of 16, then beat No. 4 Cal-Irvine, 5-1, in a mild quarterfinal upset; in the semis Georgia won its third straight 5-1 match, over TCU, which had upset No. 2 seeded UCLA, 5-4, in the quarters.

In the Stanford-Georgia finals it looked for a while that my former right-hand assistant Manuel Diaz, who had succeeded me as coach, would win the NCAA title in his first season as head coach. Al Parker won at No. 1 over the Cardinal's ace Jeff Tarango; Francisco Montana and Jim Childs won at Nos. 3 and 5; Stanford's Alex O'Brien and Barry Richards won at Nos. 4 and 6 to make the team score 3-2 for Georgia. But Martin Blackman won a long three-setter from Stephen Enochs to give Stanford a split in the singles and also the momentum. They went on to take No. 1 doubles (Tarango-O'Brien over Childs-Middleton) and No. 2 (Cathrall-Blackman over Parker-Enochs) to win their tenth NCAA team title for the redoubtable Coach Gould.

A DEPARTURE AND A RETURN

After 13 straight NCAA championships at the University of Georgia's Henry Feild Stadium, the 106th edition of this great event was played at Charley Pasarell's elegant Grand Champions' resort in Indian Wells, Ca., in May 1990.

No. 2 seed Stanford won its third straight team title, defeating No. 1 Tennessee, 5-2, in the finals, and in the process snapping the Volunteers' dual-match winning streak at 34 (a national mark for Coach Mike DePalmer's Vols).

Steve Bryan of Texas, seeded in the second four, defeated unseeded Jason Netter of UCLA in the singles finals, 6-3, 6-4. Bryan thus became the fourth Texas Longhorn to win the championship, following Wilmer Allison in 1927 and Berkeley Bell in 1929, protégés of the legendary Dr. Daniel Penick, and Kevin Curren in 1979. Both Curren and Bryan were coached by Dave Snyder.

In the doubles, Doug Eisenman and Matt Lucena of Cal-Berkeley upheld their No. 1 seed, defeating Mitch Michulka and Michael Penman of Texas in the finals, 6-3, 6-2.

The tournament returned to Athens in 1991, where Southern California's talented coach Dick Leach finally "threw the monkey off his back" by winning the NCAA team tournament he so often was picked to win after succeeding the great George Toley as Trojan chieftain in 1980.

Adding icing to the cake, his Trojans defeated their long-time nemesis, the Georgia Bulldogs, in the finals, 5-2. Georgia had beaten Coach Leach's perennial USC power-houses no less than five times in the NCAAs in Athens: 1981, '84, '85, '87 and '89.

The Trojans blanked their first two foes, Notre Dame and Florida, by 6-0 scores, then toppled No. 3 seed and defending champion Stanford, 5-2, in the semis. In the finals against

Georgia, the Trojans virtually won the match by winning four of the six singles. They lost only No. 1 when Al Parker defeated Brian MacPhie, 7-5, 7-5, and No. 4 when Bobby Mariencheck trimmed Coach Leach's son Jon Leach, 1-6, 7-6, 6-4.

Byron Black and MacPhie clinched the title by taking No. 1 doubles over Parker and Patricio Arnold, 6-2, 6-4.

Coach Manuel Diaz' Bulldogs had two thrilling but back-breaking 5-4 victories — in the quarters over No. 2 seed UCLA and in the semis over Cal-Berkeley, the latter battle ending late at night indoors. Trailing 2-4 after the singles, the fighting Bears almost won all three doubles, but Georgia's Wade McGuire and Mariencheck rallied to win No. 3 over Pete Fitzpatrick and Matt Stroyman, 6-7, 6-3, 6-3.

Stanford's Jared Palmer became the second unseeded player in 10 years to capture the singles title. (Michigan's Mike Leach — no kin to the California Leaches — won in 1982.) Palmer, a brilliant net rusher, defeated Georgia's Patricio Arnold of Argentina, who had scored three big upsets to reach the finals but then seemed to have run out of gas. Arnold had knocked off the No. 1 seed Conny Falk of Miami, No. 8 Byron Black of USC, and No. 3 Alex O'Brien of Stanford.

Georgia's Al Parker, the No. 2 seed, was toppled in the second round by Harvard's Albert Chang, 7-6, 6-2, but nevertheless went on to cap his injury-plagued collegiate career by being named the nation's outstanding collegiate player. The committee had a tough choice between the four players who had won the four so-called Grand Slam collegiate tournaments. Palmer took the NCAAs, Conny Falk of Miami the ITA-Rolex Indoors, Patricio Arnold of Georgia the ITA clay courts and Parker the Volvo All-America. Parker was chosen because he had beaten the other three in head-to-head competition that season.

California-Berkeley's wizard of a doubles player, Matt Lucena, repeated as doubles champion, this time winning with talented Norwegian Bent Pederson. In the finals they beat the No. 1 seeds, Palmer and Stark of Stanford, 6-2, 7-6 (8-6). Georgia's Wade McGuire and Bobby Mariencheck, who were fortunate to get in the draw when Tennessee's No. 4 seeded team of Tim Jessup and Brice Karsh had to withdraw because of an injury to Karsh, were surprising semifinalists but bowed to the ultimate champions Lucena and Pederson, 6-1, 6-2.

So California schools made another clean sweep of the three NCAA crowns, which they also had done in 1977, '78, '86 and '88 and were to do again in 1992.

ALEX O'BRIEN'S HAT TRICK

Stanford players swept the 1992 NCAAs — team, singles and doubles — but not a single man was a native Californian. Dick Gould's 12th NCAA championship line-up consisted of two Texans, Alex O'Brien and Michael Flanagan; two Floridians, Chris Cocotos and Jason Yee; New Yorker Robert Devens and Kentuckian Vimal Patel.

A sturdy native of Amarillo, O'Brien became the first player since the team tournament began in 1977 to pull off the "hat trick." He led The Cardinal to the coveted team title, which he followed up by impressively taking both the singles and doubles diadems, displaying a beautiful and versatile all-court game.

In the team tournament top-seeded Southern Cal, the defending champion, was upset by unseeded Notre Dame, 5-1, in the semifinals. Coach Bobby Bayliss's Irish also had toppled No. 4 seed Georgia, 5-4, in the quarters.

Seed No. 3 Stanford trampled Duke, 5-1; LSU, 5-2; No. 2 seed UCLA, 5-1, in the semis, then trounced Notre Dame, 5-0, in the finals.

In winning the singles title, O'Brien won over a tough field that included two future NCAA champions, Tennessee's Chris Woodruff (1993) and Florida's Mark Merklein (1994), and three other ITA Grand Slam singles champions: Mississippi State's Daniel Courcol, who won both the Volvo All-America and ITA Clay Courts in 1992; San Diego's Jose-Luis Noriega, winner of the ITA Clay Courts in 1989 and the Rolex Indoors in 1992; and North Carolina's Roland Thornqvist, Rolex Indoors champion in 1993.

O'Brien defeated four seeded players on consecutive days en route to his crown: Cal-Berkeley's Matt Lucena (9-16); North Carolina's Thornqvist (5-8); Noriega (No. 2) in the semis; and Georgia's Wade McGuire (5-8) in the finals, 6-3, 6-2.

It was an all-Stanford doubles finals, with the No. 2 seeds O'Brien and Cocotos trimming teammates Patel and Yee, 7-6 (7-4), 6-4. Patel and Yee, unseeded, upset the No. 1 seeds, Jon Leach and MacPhie of USC in the second round, 5-7, 6-3, 6-2. It was the ninth straight year a California school had won the doubles.

O'Brien finished his collegiate career by setting the all-time winning singles and doubles record in the NCAA since the team tournament began in 1977. He won a total of 40 matches and lost only five, counting both team and individual matches.

TENNIS UNDER THE LIGHTS IN 1993

Southeastern Conference players almost made a clean sweep of titles in the 1993 NCAAs in Athens. Tennessee's Chris Woodruff defeated Georgia's Wade McGuire in an all-SEC singles finals, Florida's Mark Merklein and David Blair took the doubles, and Georgia nearly toppled No. 1 seed Southern Cal in the team tournament finals.

A record NCAA crowd of 5,435 watched the Trojans rally to defeat hometown favorite Georgia in the first team tournament finals ever played under the lights (Kim Basinger's magnificent lighting at Henry Feild stadium).

The Bulldogs took a 3-2 lead in the singles on victories by Wade McGuire at No. 1 over Brian MacPhie, Mike Sell at No. 2 over David Ekerot and freshman Jamie Laschinger at No. 5 over Andras Lanyi; USC won at No. 3, Wayne Black over Bobby Mariencheck, and No. 6, Adam Peterson over Albin Polonyi.

At this stage, Georgia's Craig Baskin worked up to a match point against Jon Leach at No. 4, but Coach Dick Leach's youngest son rallied to score a crucial victory, 6-3, 3-6, 7-6 (7-5). The momentum swung to the Trojans, who promptly won No. 2 doubles (Black and Kent Seton over Baskin and Sell) to clinch the match, 5-3.

It was the Trojans' only hard match of the tournament. They had previously eliminated North Carolina, 5-2; Notre Dame, 5-0; and Texas, 5-0. The Bulldogs had beaten Florida, 5-0, but had to go the limit to win two fantastic cliff-hangers — in the quarters over Duke, 5-4, and the semis over No. 2 seed UCLA, 5-4. The Duke match lasted five hours and 53 minutes, but that duration was eclipsed the next day.

In the semifinals Georgia made a miraculous comeback to nip UCLA in an NCAA–record-long match (six hours and 54 minutes, including a 70-minute rain delay that forced play indoors). At No. 1 singles, McGuire was down four match points against Sebastien LeBlanc before winning, 6-4, 3-6, 7-6 (7-1), which kept Georgia alive going into the doubles. And Georgia had to win all three doubles. The Bulldogs won in straight sets at No. 2 (Laschinger-Polonyi over Sanguinetti-Sher) and at No. 3 (Sell-Baskin over Pleasant-Quinlan) to knot the team match at 4-all. Finally, McGuire-Mariencheck prevailed at No. 1 over Janecek-LeBlanc, 6-3, 5-7, 6-4.

In the singles semifinals, ultimate champion Chris Woodruff of Tennessee defeated LSU's Tamer El Sawy of Egypt, while Georgia's McGuire trimmed UCLA's David Sanguinetti. In the finals, Woodruff was red hot in downing McGuire (a finalist for the second straight year), 6-3, 6-1.

Three SEC tandems also made it to the doubles semifinals, but only one made it to the finals: champions David Blair and Mark Merklein of Florida. In the semis they defeated Juha Pesola and Mike Wesbrooks of LSU, while Stanford's Chris Cocotos and Michael Flanagan were nipping Georgia's sensational freshmen, Jamie Laschinger and Albin Polonyi, 7-6 (9-7), 7-6 (7-3). Blair and Merklein won in the finals, 5-7, 6-2, 6-1.

POSTSCRIPT

The 1994 NCAAs were held at Notre Dame, where the tournament had also taken place in 1971. Southern California defeated Stanford to repeat as team champion. Florida's Mark Merklein upset No. 1 seed Wayne Black of USC in the singles finals, 6-2, 6-7 (10-8), 6-4. In the doubles finals Mississippi State's Lauren Miquelard (France) and Joc Simmons toppled the No. 3 seeds, Black and Jon Leach of USC, 7-6 (7-5), 2-6, 6-3.

We are delighted that the championships have been contracted to return to Athens in 1995 and 1996.

"Aftermath"

Georgia's success in tennis is largely due to our magnificent "support troops," and there is no way I can adequately express my profound appreciation to all of them. Heading this group are our ever-loyal lettermen and a battalion of staunch friends, many of whom have contributed generously in the financing of projects that have made our complex perhaps the finest collegiate layout in the country.

Also of vital importance are the Athens lady volunteers who are the real "hosts" of the NCAAs, with their work as stadium ushers, program and concessions sellers, transporters and party-planners for the players and visiting fans. Some have chaired these crucial committees for years: Maxine Davis, Sharon Warren, Joanne Sinkey, Gwen Griffin, Jane McMullan, Jinx Baldwin, Cathy Whitworth and Hildegarde Timberlake.

And special thanks to my secretaries through the years: Ann Frierson, Harriett Chambers, Grace Gaby, Vivian Nickerson, Mary Lou McCormick, Christine West and Laura Rockwell. Vivian, although retired, still helps us as chair of our important ticket sales drive, and a few years ago she received a special award from the NCAA for her outstanding service.

Our UGA sports information staff does yeoman work each year at the NCAAs. Thank you, Director Claude Felton and Assistant Norm Reilly. Ditto our training staff under the direction of recently retired Warren Morris and his successor, Steve Bryant. And hats off to our expert gardener, Kellie

Baxter, and veteran groundskeeper James Payne, who get many compliments throughout the year for maintaining our complex so admirably.

Most of our lettermen's support has come from my own former players, but three old-timers have been of much assistance: John (Judge) Beaver of Gainesville, Ga., and Fort Lauderdale, Fla., our captain in 1932; Judge Aaron Cohn of Columbus, Ga., captain in '36; and the late Major General Albert Jones of Athens, captain in '37 and tennis coach from 1949 to 1954. Albert and I were sparring partners for many years, as were our sons (Albert Jr. and Ham) and daughters (his Sydney and my Sharon), and our granddaughters (Sydney Flournoy of Columbus and Cathleen Magill of Athens) — three generations!

Two other unsung heroes of our program are lifelong friends Art Prochaska, an ex-Marine buddy of Fort Lauderdale, and Jack Waters, veteran pro at Atlanta's Piedmont Driving Club. They "sent" me nearly two dozen of my best players. Art had been a tennis star at little Presbyterian College under the great coach Bill Lufler, and had also been Gardnar Mulloy's doubles partner before World War II. He certainly knew a good prospect when he saw one. Seven of his Florida boys — Norm Holmes, Mike Cmaylo, Bill Kopecky, Brant Bailey, Joe Gettys, Tom Foster and George Bezecny — made All-SEC; and Holmes, Kopecky and Bezecny made All-America. Seven of Jack Waters' protégés became Georgia captains: Lindsey Hopkins III, Charley Benedict, Thomas Benedict, Carleton Fuller, Bill Shippey, Rocky Huffman and Philip Johnson.

I am as indebted to my non-scholarship teams as I am to those who garnered the laurel wreaths, especially the 1960 team that I thought would be good enough to challenge mighty Tulane for the SEC title. Unfortunately, this team lost three of its six members when the spring quarter began, and I even considered canceling the schedule. Instead I put a desperate ad in the school newspaper, begging for any student with high school tennis experience, and three players came to the rescue: Zuhair Nejib from Iraq; Guy Arnall, a good intramural tennis player who had played football in high school; and Hill Griffin, who two years later won the SEC No. 5 singles and is today one of the nation's top senior players. These walk-ons, plus regulars Joe Manderson, Scott Henson and Charles (Buzzy) Cowart, amazingly finished fifth in the 12-team conference tournament.

I am also deeply appreciative of the team that produced Georgia's first-ever SEC tennis champions. You can imagine how happy we were in 1961 down in Gainesville, Fla., when these non-scholarshipped players broke the ice: Charley Bryan at No. 3 singles, who jumped flat-footed over the hood of our car in celebration on the ride back home; Charley Benedict at No. 4 (who, along with younger brother Thomas, had such a great forehand that we named our Forehand Award for them); Comer Hobbs at No. 6; and Benedict and Buzzy Cowart at No. 3 doubles.

I'll always have especially fond memories of the nine foreign players I had during my 34 years as Georgia's coach, though I didn't go out and recruit a single one of them. They were all good players and fine boys, and most of them could speak better English than I. In fact, I could understand their English much better than they could my Southern drawl.

I've already written about the royal Zuhair Nejib of Baghdad, little Elango Ranganathan of India, and our wonderful Swedes Ola Malmqvist and Mikael Pernfors. Freddie Sauer, an All-American at Miami, telephoned me from South Africa to recommend his younger brother Kosie; and former captain Norm Holmes, while teaching in Graz, Austria, recommended Gerald Thonhauser of Vienna. Jack Waters sent Marko Ostoja, a Yugoslavian, who played one quarter before turning pro.

My Aussies, Peter Lloyd and Stephen Maloney, were recommended by none other than the distinguished United States Ambassador to Australia, Georgia alumnus Phillip Alston of Atlanta. I'll never forget his call from Australia, informing me that we could have the Australian boys' champion if we wanted him. Furthermore, he said the boy was coached by the great Charlie Hollis (who had coached Rod Laver) and that he was the son of the head gardener at the American embassy in Canberra. His name was Peter Lloyd, and he proved to be one of the best players in Georgia history, helping us win SEC titles in 1979, '81 and '82.

Peter was also a super doubles player, so good that in 1982, although Allen Miller and Ola Malmqvist were finalists in the NCAAs, I nevertheless gave our David Dick Doubles Award to Lloyd, who now is a very successful teaching pro in Atlanta.

A very special part of my good fortune was to have had an unusually large number of straight-A students on my teams through the years, starting with the very first one in 1955 right up to the last one in 1988 — which happened to set the university men's athletic team record for highest grade point average. The best thing about having smart boys was that they could remember my instructions better than the "dumbos," of which I was one when I was in school.

My first team in '55 had three outstanding students, all of whom went on to become teachers: Captain Bill McMullan, who majored in veterinary medicine and is now at Texas A & M; my first cousin Merritt Pound, Jr., whose father was head of the university's political science department and who himself returned to his alma mater, after a distinguished Air

Force career, to head the university's AF ROTC detachment; and Danny Huff, whose father headed out mathematics department and who teaches history in Beaufort, S.C. Danny's father, incidentally, was a star player and one-time tennis coach at Southern Methodist.

My very "smartest" team compiled a grade point average of 3.35 for the entire school year of 1987-88, and that mark still stands as the highest of any men's athletic team in university annals. Its No. 1 "brain," freshman Al Parker, was also our No. 1 player. He had a 4.0 average, as he did his entire career on the way to becoming his class's valedictorian. Jim Childs and Stephen Enochs were on that team, too, and they often had perfect 4.0 averages for a quarter's work. In fact, Childs graduated with a 3.99 average and is now at the Harvard Graduate School of Business.

Appreciating the outstanding academic work of our players through the years just as much as I did was Dr. Lothar Tresp, head of the university's honors program and for 40 years one of our most loyal fans and supporters. Lothar especially liked to brag to the faculty that "his tennis players" were so often among the school's top students.

While given the opportunity, I cannot fail to mention my special pride and joy: the Eugene Dykes Memorial Garden, named for my late classmate and fellow swim team member, "Newt" Dykes of Columbus, Ga. Among the friends who have made this wonderful garden possible are Newt's wife Betty Dykes; Frank and Sally Foley and Frank Lumpkin of Columbus; and Tom Pendergrast and Arthur Montgomery of Atlanta. I'm happy to say that UGA's renowned horticulturists Dr. Gary Couvillon, Dr. Michael Dirr and Dr. Allan Armitage are now in on the project, and it won't be long before our garden is prettier than the Garden of Eden.

In looking back over my tennis days at Georgia, I must say I have few regrets. But I can think of two. First, if Zahner Reynolds of Atlanta, captain of our 1941 team, had come along after we had begun emphasizing tennis with year-round play under an actual coach, I believe he would have made All-America. Trey Carter had our most spectacular forehand drive, but Zahner (also a super athlete) had the most beautifully stroked forehand, hit with the Eastern grip of Big Bill Tilden. And second, if Tina Price of Dublin, Ga., the best athlete ever to play women's tennis at Georgia, had concentrated solely on tennis instead of playing basketball as well during her tenure in the mid-1970s, she could have become our first women's All-American.

Of course, weighed against 34 years of wonderful memories and more success than I ever hoped for (or deserved), that's not a lot to be sorry for.

Index

Bold numbers indicate photographs.